PRAISE FOR SEARCHING FOR GOD KNOWS WHAT

"Miller . . . writes on faith with candor and passion reminiscent of Frederick Buechner and Anne Lamott."

—*The Oregonian*

"Like a shaken snow globe, Donald Miller's newest collection of essays creates a swirl of ideas about the Christian life that eventually crystallize into a lovely landscape . . . [He] is one of the evangelical book market's most creative writers."

—*Christianity Today*

"For fans of *Blue Like Jazz*, I doubt you will be disappointed. Donald Miller writes with the wit and vulnerability that you expect. Sharing stories of his upbringing and his journey in more recent years, he perfectly illustrates important themes in a genuine and humorous manner . . . For those who would be reading Miller for the first time, this would be a great start."

—*Relevant*

"We need this book. It demonstrates that when Christianity is articulated with intelligence, it proves viable to those of us in the academic community."

—Tony Campolo
Professor of Sociology, Eastern University
and Author of *Speaking My Mind*

"If you have felt that Jesus is someone you respect and admire—but Christianity is something that repels you—*Searching for God Knows What* will give you hope that you still can follow Jesus and be part of a church without the trappings of organized religion."

—Dan Kimball
Author of *The Emerging Church*
and Pastor of Vintage Faith Church, Santa Cruz, CA

"In *Searching for God Knows What,* Donald Miller cuts through the temptation of looking for how-to's and formulas to bring us life. Instead, he reveals a refreshingly simple and beautiful look at why we were created—to be in relationship first with our Creator and then with our neighbors. What a refreshing reminder of what Christ came to accomplish on this earth. Thanks, Donald, for being bold enough to tell us not what we *want* to hear, but rather what we *need* to hear."

—Charlie Lowell
Band Member, Jars of Clay

"Once again, Donald Miller reminds us that living Christ is not a twelve-step recovery program from the real world . . . but rather an invitation into its middle. *Searching for God Knows What* shows us that life is an invitation to follow Jesus into the corner of the world each of us has been given and to simply love the people we find there."

—Bebo Norman
Singer/Songwriter, *Myself When I Am Real* and *Try*

"Whenever people ask me about Donald Miller, I notice the first thing I say is, 'That guy can write.' Having met Don, I also know he seeks to live what he writes, or better said, he writes what he lives. That, I think, is the top credential for a person who writes about ultimate concerns—spirituality, meaning, purpose, life, God, and joy. In *Searching for God Knows What,* you'll find more of his great writing, honest feeling, and spiritual insight to help you on your journey."

—Brian McLaren
Pastor, Author—www.anewkindofchristian.com

"In *Searching for God Knows What,* Donald Miller combines Bob Dylan's no-nonsense message of the good news in *Slow Train Coming* with Søren Kierkegaard's attack on dead orthodoxy in a fresh style and compelling form. Miller helps spiritual seekers get beyond those doctrinal rules and religious and political traditions that cloud the real Jesus and helps 'churchians' rediscover Jesus Christ as their first love."

—Paul Louis Metzger
Associate Professor, Multnomah Biblical Seminary
and Author of *The Word of Christ and the World of Culture*

SEARCHING FOR GOD KNOWS WHAT

DONALD MILLER

THOMAS NELSON
Since 1798

NASHVILLE DALLAS MEXICO CITY RIO DE JANEIRO

Published in Nashville, Tennessee, by Thomas Nelson. Thomas Nelson is a registered trademark of Thomas Nelson, Inc.

Thomas Nelson, Inc. books may be purchased in bulk for educational, business, fund-raising, or sales promotional use. For information, please e-mail SpecialMarkets@ThomasNelson.com.

ISBN 978-1-4002-0275-1 (repackage)

Library of Congress Cataloging-in-Publication Data

Miller, Donald, 1971–
Searching for God knows what / Donald Miller.
p. cm.
ISBN 978-0-7852-6371-5
1. Miller, Donald, 1971– 2. Christian biography—United States. 3. Christian life—Miscellanea. I. Title.
BR1725.M4465A3 2004
277.3'082'092—dc22

2004014208

Printed in the United States of America
13 14 QG 8

This book is dedicated to
John MacMurray.

A NOTE ABOUT THIS BOOK

Dear Reader, as you enjoy this book, you will encounter some small irregularities on various pages, things like bolded letters, randomly occurring numbers, and more. They are there on purpose and invite you into a game to find God knows what. At the back of this book, you will find game instructions and a decoder wheel that you can use to unlock secret content from Donald Miller and become eligible to win prizes.

The official Searching for God Knows What game begins June 2010 and lasts for eight weeks. If you're reading this after that time or if you are using an eReader, you still have the chance to play! You can go to these websites to retrieve all the clues you need and still receive prizes and secret content.

www.DonaldMillerFan.com

and

www.SearchingForGodKnowsWhat.com

CONTENTS

AUTHOR'S NOTE

Sometimes I feel as though I were born in a circus, come out of my mother's womb like a man from a cannon, pitched toward the ceiling of the tent, all the doctors and nurses clapping in delight from the grandstands, the band going great guns in trombones and drums. I unfold and find flight hundreds of feet above the center ring, the smell of popcorn in the air, the clowns gather below, amazed at my grace, and all the people chanting my name as my arms come out like wings and I move swan-like toward the apex, where I draw my arms in, collapse my torso to my legs, roll over in perfection, then slowly give in to gravity. My body falls back toward earth, the ground coming up quick, the center ring growing enormous beneath my falling weight.

And this is precisely when it occurs to me that there is no net. And I wonder, *What is the use of a circus?* and *Why should a man bother to be shot out of a cannon? and Why is the crowd's applause so fleeting?* and . . . *Who is going to rescue me?*

INTRODUCTION

I wrote *Searching for God Knows What* just after turning in *Blue Like Jazz.* That book took a year to get legs, so at the time I was still a struggling writer talking to myself. It was a great season, looking back. I was living with five other guys, barely able to make rent, sharing life and faith, and to some degree, figuring out what life and faith were all about.

I'd grown up in a very conservative, Southern Baptist church in Texas. Urban living in Portland stood in stark contrast. Portland, and for that matter the Pacific Northwest in general, is not a place where Christian faith is a social commodity. In other parts of the country, people go to church for community, and while their faith may be genuine, there are other benefits to being with the body of Christ, social benefits that may go unnoticed but are certainly there and in abundance.

A person can advance in their career by being a Christian; they can meet a soul mate from a large pool of Christian singles; they can gain social acceptance in their culture by displaying a stable spiritual life. This doesn't happen in Portland. In fact, it's much the opposite. Being a Christian can cost you. It's a liberal, progressive community. There are dark elements, to be sure, as Portland was recently selected as the most depressed city in the country. But it's a terrific culture, too, also selected as the number-one city in which to live. It's a well-read city, one of the more literary cities in the country, that breeds a level of worldly sophistication which, when compared to the self-help tendency of the average Christian communicator, seems more sophisticated on the outside.

As a side note, I don't think that criticism is exactly fair. We live in a constant self-help movement, where trite sayings are sold as life-guiding philosophy. Christians have adopted this technique, to be sure, only proving their finds with hand-picked Bible verses. But the church also has a smaller, richer intellectual history that is alive and well, thriving even. It's no different than mass culture, in that sense, in that mass culture has an intellectual crowd and a self-help crowd and one is obviously larger than the other. The secular sophisticate will compare their intellectual life to the self-help life of the average Christian, then, and the comparison isn't exactly fair. One would need to compare the two intellectual components to be more accurate. But this is neither here nor there.

What I'm getting at is the sophisticated literary culture I found in Portland began to clash with the simple answers I'd learned growing up in church. In fact, in the southeast, you could hide from any threat to your faith because Christian culture is so vast. Kids can go to a Christian school; young adults, to a Christian university; adults, to a Christian company. You can find a wife at a Christian church, have kids, and reset the cycle by putting your kids in a Christian school. You could live within the giant walls of M. Night Shyamalan's village, making an enemy of the outside world that doesn't believe in you. Such a fantasy life is not possible in Portland. You must mix and mingle and have your faith rub against antagonists.

Without realizing it, my simple answers were being threatened. I had come to believe there was a right theology (which I still believe) and this right theology would redeem me (which I no longer believe). The culture I was in allowed me to see how simple and naive my faith had become, and not only simple and naïve, but counter to the sophisticated, remarkably beautiful, and profound precepts of Scripture. The Bible was not saying what I'd grown up believing it said, and that was fine, because what I thought it was saying would fall apart under even the simplest of intellectual scrutiny. What it was saying, perhaps, was more profound and relevant than a safe Christian culture taught me to believe and understand.

But this revelation wasn't like a lightbulb coming on. It was more like giving birth, with lots of pain and muck and fear. The inciting incident came with a simple question: How does a person become a Christian? I always had a readymade answer: they believe in Jesus. But living in Portland, I also knew a lot of people who believed in Jesus, but they also believed other faiths and, well, aliens and the Easter Bunny and all the rest. So I thought there must be a qualifier to faith, that there must be some theological list a person must understand. When I drew up this list of ideas, I realized the ideas would not be accessible to the simple thinker, that those who were not as intelligent, or perhaps children, would not be able to be Christians. And that's when the fear and trembling set in. I had painted myself into a corner. The answer to how a person becomes Christians could not be intellectual, it had to be something else.

And through a dark night of the soul, I came to realize that salvation happens through a mysterious, indefinable, relational interaction with Jesus in which we become one with Him. I realized Christian conversion worked more like falling in love than understanding a series of concepts or ideas. This is not to say there are no true ideas, it is only to say there is something else, something beyond. There are true ideas involved in marriage and sex, but marriage and sex also involve something else, and that something else is mysterious.

If we have a controlling personality, in which we like to check things off of lists, this is going to be extremely hard for us to understand and embrace. God gives us no control, really, over this "system" of relationship. Introducing somebody to Jesus is not about presenting ideas, then, as much as it is introducing a person to a Deity who lives and interacts. Evangelism, then, looks like setting somebody up on a blind date: God does the work, we just tell them about Him and where they can find Him.

You might be getting upset by this. You might think I am saying truth should be thrown out, that theology doesn't matter. But this is not what I'm saying at all. What I'm intending to illustrate is that our drive to define God with a mathematical theology has become a false God rather than an arrow that points to the real God. Theology can become an idol, but it is more useful as guardrails on a road to the true God. Theology is very important, but it is not God, and knowing facts about God is not the same as knowing God. Let me give you an extreme example of how very bad we have gotten about this in the West.

About the time (and I share this in the book, so forgive the repetition) I was thinking through these things, I was teaching a class in Canada, and my students were freshman college students, all of whom had grown up in the church. The class was called "The Gospel and Culture." I started the class with an experiment. I told the class I was going to share the gospel of Jesus, but I was going to leave something out. I wanted them to figure out what I'd left out. I talked first about sin, about how we are fallen creatures. I told some stories and used some illustrations. I talked about repentance, and again told some stories, then I talked about God's forgiveness, and I talked about heaven. I went on for some time. And when I finally stopped and asked the class to tell me what I'd left out, after twenty or more minutes of discussion, not one student realized I'd left out *Jesus.* Not one. And I believe I could repeat that same experiment in Christian classrooms across North America.

What I came to understand, then, is Christian conversion is *relational*. It is not theological or intellectual any more than marriage is theological or intellectual. In other words, a child could become a Christian if they had a mysterious encounter with Jesus, and a simple thinker could become a Christian if they had a mysterious encounter with Christ, and even a person who was a Muslim or a Buddhist could become a Christian if they had a mysterious relational encounter with Christ. This is the only answer at which I could arrive that matched the reality in which we live, the complexity of Scripture, and the mysterious invitation offered to us by Jesus.

I hear the masses saying, "But no! A person cannot believe in multiple Gods and be a Christian." Let me counter with some questions:

Can a person have bad theology and be a Christian?

Has your theology ever been corrected, and were you really a Christian before?

Is your theology all worked out now so you have no more reason to study, and if not, are you a Christian?

If you believe a person's theology has to be right for him or her to be qualified for Christian conversion, then you are saying a person comes to know God, in part, because he has right ideas, and I respectfully disagree. Do I think right theology is important? Absolutely, but I do not believe it has any agency to convert any more than directions to the doctor's office have the power to heal.

I have a friend who countered, adamantly, that unless a person understood and agreed with the theological idea of total depravity, he could not be a Christian. I asked my friend when it was that he understood the idea himself, and he answered his sophomore year in seminary. I asked him, then, when he had become a Christian, and he told me when he was in the third grade. His reasoning was obviously insane, and I don't think he is alone. I believe that God wants us to engage with and be transformed by His Word. So does that mean someone from another faith who encounters Jesus might have their ideology corrected? Maybe. What I'm saying, though, is that God doesn't exclude someone from His saving grace because they don't have the correct theological checklist. And for those of us who judge and condemn them, why would we stand in opposition when the God we love and serve is Himself so adamant about being in relationship with them just as He is with us?

Would you do me a favor as you read this book? Would you be willing to grow and expand your understanding of God and how He works? If your understanding of Christianity is relatively conservative, it may surprise you that our theology is remarkably similar. It's just that I am going to continue to pull power and beauty away from facts about God and give them to God Himself. To the degree your right theology is your false God, this is going to disturb you. You are going to revolt, inside, because the thing you have been placing your security in (namely your ability to come up with and defend right ideas) is going to be threatened. But make no mistake, I am not attacking right theology, I am simply making theology a window rather than a wall.

On this journey, you may travel through the same dark night of the soul through which I have come. But on the other side, I assure you, is Christ, and you will love Him for what He has done. You will stand bloodied from the battle, kneeling before Him, knowing He is all the hope you had, and hopefully, in a delightful moment of freedom, realize He is always the only hope you need.

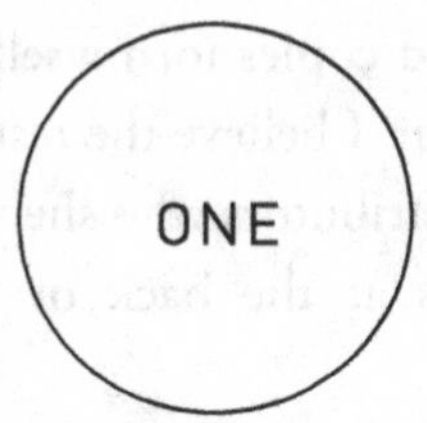

Fine Wine

The Failure of Formulas

Some time ago I attended a seminar for Christian writers. It was in a big hotel down South and hotels always make me uncomfortable because the bedding is so fluffy and the television swivels, and who makes coffee in the bathroom? But I felt that I needed to be at this seminar. I was wondering how, exactly, to write a book for a Christian market, a book that people would actually read. I had written a book several years before, but it didn't sell. It was a road-trip narrative about me, a friend, and God, and how we traveled across the country in a Volkswagen van, smoking pipes and picking fights with truckers. God wasn't actually a character in the book the way my friend and I were; God more or less played Himself, up in heaven, sending down puzzling wisdom and answers to prayer every hundred miles or so.

But even though the story had God in it, which I believed made it prime for Christian bookstores, sales were less than holy. The book limped along for about a year and then, suddenly, died. God led the publisher to take the book out of print about the same time sales dipped into negative figures. The publisher called and asked if I wanted to buy a few thousand copies for myself at twelve cents each and I ended up buying four. I believe the rest of the books were sold to convenience-store distributors who shelved them next to three-dollar romance novels at the back of the potato-chip aisle.

The only positive thing that happened in all this was that for the next year or so I received enjoyable and sultry e-mails from women who had recently begun to consider themselves spiritual. And while I certainly enjoyed the correspondence and still keep in touch with many of these women today, the career path was not as respectable as I would have liked. I have always wanted to be a sophisticated Christian writer and not somebody who has books on the close-out aisle at Plaid Pantry. That is why I signed up for this seminar, the one I was telling you about that was in the hotel with the bathroom/cafés.

I arrived the evening before, and so the morning of the seminar I woke up very early, about six, and I couldn't fall back to sleep. I opened the curtains and watched planes land at the Memphis airport for an hour or so, trying to guide them in with my mind and that sort of thing. And then I went into the bathroom and sat down and had some coffee and read the paper. After an hour I started getting dressed, and the whole time I was ironing my clothes I was wondering whether this would be the weekend I would be discovered, whether this would be the start of a long career writing adventurous, life-changing books for my fellow brothers and sisters in Christ. I sat on the edge of the bed in my suit and tie and watched television for an hour. Katie Couric was interviewing a fellow who had written a book about how Donald Rumsfeld was actually the Antichrist and I confess, I practiced answering all her questions, knowing that I, too, would some day be interviewed by Katie Couric:

You really make Mr. Rumsfeld out to be a monster, Mr. Miller. This seems unfounded. How did you come to these conclusions?

I had him followed by a private detective, a high-tech guy I found at Radio Shack. Everything in the book is documented, Miss Couric. Or may I call you Katie? Or may I just call you?

When the interview was over I turned the television off and lay back on the fluffy bed and stared at the bedside clock, trying to speed up time with my mind, but time went on as usual and so I fell asleep for exactly nine minutes and then woke up and tried not to blink till about twenty minutes to eight, which is when I headed downstairs. In the lobby I asked the man at the front desk which room the seminar was in. I leaned against the desk as the concierge, a twenty-something fellow with a goatee, searched for a room schedule among his papers. "Capturing literature for the glory of God?" the man asked suspiciously, reading the name of the seminar from a sheet of paper, looking up at me as if to ask whether or not this was the seminar I was interested in and also, perhaps, why God was trying to "capture literature for His glory." "That's the one," I said to him. "Interesting name for a conference, isn't it?" he said, looking at me with a smile.

"We can't have literature running around doing anything it wants now, can we?" I told him.

"I don't suppose so," he said after a long and uncomfortable pause.

"And where will we be capturing said literature?" I asked. By this I was asking what room we were in. He looked at me, puzzled. "What room are we in?" I clarified.

"Oh," he said as he looked back at the sheet. "You are in conference room 210, which is just down the hall across from the restrooms."

"Perfect," I said, adding that if he saw people in the lobby reading pagan literature to please notify me.

"Certainly," he said to me, confused, but kind of standing at attention all the same.

I remember having a very good feeling that morning, walking down the big hall toward the conference room, once again believing I was on my way to becoming the next great spiritual writer, a sort of evangelical Deepak Chopra crossed with Tom Clancy, or that guy who wrote *Jonathan Livingston Seagull,* or Ansel Adams, or whoever, just somebody famous. I had terrific ideas; I really did. I was going to write a story about a nun who takes over small third-world countries by causing their evil dictators to fall in love with her, leaving a trail of megachurches and democracy in her wake. The book was going to be called *Sister Democracy, Show Some Leg!*

I had another story about a guy whose father, a psychology professor at a prestigious university, raised his son in a maze, rewarding him when he crawled down dark hallways and disciplining him when he crawled down lit hallways, thus teaching him to do everything in life counterintuitively. In the story, the kid grows up to be a kind of genius with an enormous following; people hanging on his every word. The book was going to be called *Maze Boy: How One Man Brought Down the United States Postal Service!* And if it were a Christian novel, and I could easily turn it into a Christian novel if the money was right, I was going to call it *Maze Boy: How One Man, with God's Help, Brought Down the United States Postal Service!*

I stocked up on bagels at the back of the conference room because I was the first one there. I chose a chair somewhere near the middle, and soon fellow writers began shuffling in, perhaps twenty or so over the next ten minutes. Everybody was being very quiet, looking over their notebooks, but I made small talk with a woman next to me about why we were there and where we had come from and what sort of books we liked to read. Some of the nicest people you could ever hope to meet will be at a Christian writers seminar, I'll tell you that right now. Very small people, though, mostly women, not the sort of folks you would imagine taking literature captive for the glory of God, but kind and others-centered nonetheless.

The lady sitting next to me was writing a wonderful series of Christian devotionals for girls who were taking ballet classes, and the lady on the other side of me was writing a series of devotionals you could read while drinking tea. When she told me this, a lady in front of us turned around and smiled because she was working on a series of devotionals you could read while drinking coffee. I told them their books sounded terrific, because it is true that some people like tea and some people like coffee, and for that matter, some people dance in ballets.

The ladies asked me what I was working on, and I told them about the nun in South America and described a specific scene in which the nun actually ponders whether or not *she* has fallen in love with a dictator named Pablo Hernandez-Juarez, and I had the ladies lean in as I told them the part where the nun is standing on a balcony overlooking a Pacific sunset, painfully considering whether she should go back inside to be with Pablo or whether she should scale the side of the dictator's castle, thus escaping to move on to the next country, the next dictator, and the next story of passion and liberation. You could tell the ladies really liked my story, and all three of them told me it was a terrific idea. I told them about how, in my mind, it was actually a musical, and I whistled a few bars from the love theme. I was going to tell them about the kid who grew up in a maze and brought down the United States Postal Service, but that's when the lady who was going to teach the seminar showed up.

She was also a small woman, but she knew her stuff. Three of her books had been published: a series of devotionals you could read while eating chocolate, a book about the hidden secrets of fulfillment found in end-times prophecy, and a book about how to make "big money" painting "small houses." Three different genres, she told us, but each one had been a success. She told us that there are, in fact, formulas for writing successful books, and that if we followed one of these formulas, we, too, could write books that end up on subcategory Christian or Catholic bestseller lists, not the monthly ones, but the annual ones, which also consider backlist titles and total sales, including sales to ministries and radio stations as promotional giveaways. Of course I was interested, and I elbowed the lady next to me and lifted my eyebrows.

"The first formula goes like this," our seminar instructor began, holding a finger in the air. "You begin with a crisis. This can be a global crisis, a community crisis, whatever kind of crisis you want. This isn't a *problem*, or a *nuisance*, mind you, this is a *crisis*. This must be something terrible that is going to happen to the world, to our country, to the church, or to the individual unless the reader does something about it. The reader must be taken to the point where they fear the consequences of this crisis. Second, there must be a clear enemy in the crisis, some group of people or some person or some philosophy that is causing the crisis. You must show examples of how these people are causing this crisis, simply because they are the enemy of all that is good. Third, you must spell out the ramifications of the crisis should it go unchecked, and also the glory and beauty of the crisis if dealt with. You must paint a picture of a war against evil forces that are trying to cause this crisis, and you must enlist the reader in this war, painting a very clear picture of the reader as the good guy in the war against the crisis. Fourth, and finally, you must spell out a three- to four-step plan of dealing with said crisis." And with this she took a breath. "Is that clear?" she asked, and as she delivered this last line, she more or less stood up straight, her petite frame putting out the confident vibe of a drill sergeant. I knew, then and there, that these were the women *to take literature captive for the glory of God*, and that, in fact, standing before me was the archetype of my South American nun. But as excited as I was, I confess I began to wonder how I was going to work this formula into *Sister of Democracy, Show Some Leg!* or *Maze Boy: How One Man Brought Down the United States Postal Service!*

"Now, there is another recipe!" she said, which gave me hope that there might be a more compatible formula for one of my stories. "First," she began, "you must paint a picture of great personal misery. You must tell the reader of a time when you failed at something, when you had no control over a situation or dynamic. Second, you must talk about where you are now, and how you have control over that situation or dynamic, and how wonderful and fulfilling it is to have control. Third, you must give the reader a three- to four-step plan for getting from the misery and lack of control to the joy and control you currently have."

As wonderful as I thought this formula was, and I confess that I thought it was wonderful, once again I felt that it was going to be difficult for me to wrap a story around one of these recipes. I thought perhaps there would be another formula, perhaps one with guns or a midnight parachute drop into a small African village, but there wasn't. It turns out there were only two formulas. Our instructor went on to tell us that during the next two days, for eight hours each day, we were going to walk step-by-step through these two magical formulas, and by the end of our time we were going to have them mastered; that, essentially, we would be able to approach any topic and *hook* the reader from the very first paragraph.

I sat and listened attentively, taking copious notes, learning to *look for the misery that is hiding beneath the surface of life, the misery that many people will not feel until you tell them it is there,* and to *identify the joy we now feel because the misery has been overcome by taking three steps,* and how *these three steps are very easy and can be taken by anybody who has fifteen dollars to spend on my book.*

When it came time for lunch, I let the room empty out except for our seminar instructor, and feeling defeated and confused because I didn't believe these formulas were necessarily compatible with my stories, I approached her and asked about how I might fit one of these formulas into a book about a nun with a machete. She looked over my shoulder into the empty room, tilted her head, then looked back into my eyes and asked whether I realized this was a *nonfiction* rather than a *fiction* seminar. At the time, I confess, I didn't know the difference between *fiction* and *nonfiction,* so I slyly inquired about the delineation. "What," I began, "do you feel is the largest difference between a work of *fiction* and a work of *nonfiction*?" And again she looked at me, confused. "Well," she said, "I suppose a nonfiction book would be *true*, and a fiction book would be *made up.*"

"For example . . . ," I said, motioning with my hand for an example.

"Well," she began, looking at the floor and smiling before looking back at me, kind of sighing as she spoke, "a novel, a story like the one you are talking about, would be considered a fiction book. But a self-help book, the sort of book we are discussing at this seminar, would be considered nonfiction, because we aren't really making up stories so much as we are trying to offer advice."

"I see," I said, kind of looking at the ceiling.

"I get it," I said, looking back at the floor.

"Indeed," I said, looking back at my instructor.

"Does that help?" she asked, smiling and putting her hand on my arm.

"It does," I said. "It helps a great deal. I like to get people's perspective on fiction and nonfiction. I find the various opinions intriguing."

"I am sure you do," she said to me after a long and uncomfortable pause.

I ate lunch at the Denny's across the street from the hotel, feeling the entire trip to Memphis had been a mistake. And then I remembered a little song, something about making lemons from a lemon tree, and I realized that what I needed to do was write a nonfiction book, something that helped people who were miserable become happy. Only mine would be a Christian self-help book, and I would start each reading with Scripture, then break down the formula the Scripture spoke of. I would call it *Devotions You Can Read While Eating Ice Cream, Soy Ice Cream, and So On!*

There is no question I was the best student at this seminar. Women under one hundred pounds lose energy in the late afternoons because they do not eat enough and they miss their families. I returned home and began poring over the Bible, looking for formulas I could use for my book of daily devotions. And I have to tell you this was much more difficult than you might think. The formulas, in fact, are hidden. It seems when God had the Bible put together, He hid a lot of the ancient wisdom so, basically, you have to read into things and even kind of make up things to get a formula out of it. And the formulas that are obvious are terrible.

For instance, a guy named Stephen was miserable (or at least I assumed he was miserable) and then he became a Christian, and then he was stoned to death. This formula, of course, was not good enough to make the cut. And for that matter, neither was the one about Paul, who was a murderer before he became a Christian and then was blinded while traveling, met Jesus in a burst of light, and then spent various painful years moving from city to city, prison to prison, routinely being beaten and bitten by snakes. No formula there. I moved on to Peter, who was rescued from a successful fishing business only to be crucified, some historical accounts claim, along with his wife. And of course that wouldn't work. So I decided to ignore the actual characters of Scripture and just go with the teachings of Jesus. And that is when things really became difficult. Apparently Jesus had not heard of the wonderful tool of acronyms. He mostly told stories, some of which were outlandish. Step one: Eat My flesh. Step two: Drink My blood. Do you know what having to read something like that would do to a guy trying to process dairy products?

Of course, I got frustrated. And it really got me thinking that, perhaps, formula books, and by that I mean books that take you through a series of steps, may not be all that compatible with the Bible. I looked on my shelf at all the self-help books I happened to own, the ones about losing weight, the ones about making girls like you, the ones about getting rich, the ones about starting your own pirate radio station, and I realized none of them actually helped me all that much. All the promises of fulfillment really didn't work. My life was fairly normal before I read them, meaning I had good days and bad days, and then my life was fairly normal after I read them too, meaning I still had good days and bad days. It made me wonder, honestly, if such a complex existence as the one you and I are living can really be broken down into a few steps. It seems if there were a formula to fix life, Jesus would have told us what it was.

A few weeks later I learned an invaluable lesson from a wealthy and successful businessman here in Portland who owns a chain of coffee shops. A few of us were sitting in one of his shops one morning, and another friend asked if we had seen the World Series of Poker on television the night before. None of us had, but that mention led to a conversation about gambling. My friend who owns the coffee shops told us, in a tone of kindness and truth, that nobody he knows who is successful gambles; rather, they work hard, they accept the facts of reality, they enjoy life as it is. "But the facts of reality stink," I told him. "Reality is like a fine wine," he said to me. "It will not appeal to children." And I am grateful my friend stung me in that way, because this truth helped me understand and appreciate life itself, as it is, without the false hope formulas offer. I didn't read formula books after that because reality is like fine wine. I am quite snobby about it, if you want to know the truth.

That said, I do believe people change, and I do believe life can get better. I have changed, slowly and with time, the way a tree grows by a river. I have a very intelligent and conservative friend who teaches at a local Bible college, and he believes the only thing that truly changes a person is God's truth, that is, His Word and His working in our lives through the Holy Spirit. This makes a lot of sense to me, because the times in my life when I have been most happy haven't been the times when I've had the most money or the most freedom or the most anything, but rather when I've been in love or in community or right with people.

My friend at the Bible college believes the qualities that improve a person's life are relational, relational to God and to the folks around us. This made a lot of sense, too, because when Jesus was walking around on earth He taught His disciples truths through experience, first telling them stories, then walking with them, then causing stuff to happen like a storm on the sea, then reiterating the idea He had taught them the day before. Even then it took years before the disciples understood, and even then the Holy Spirit had to come and wrap things up. So it made me realize that either God didn't know about the formulas, or the formulas weren't able to change a person's heart.

To be honest, though, I don't know how much I like the idea of my spirituality being relational. I suppose I believe this is true, but the formulas seem much better than God because the formulas offer control; and God, well, He is like a person, and people, as we all know, are complicated. The trouble with people is they do not always do what you tell them to do. Try it with your kids or your spouse or strangers at the grocery store, and you will see what I mean. The formulas propose that if you do this and this and this, God will respond. When I was a kid I wanted a dolphin for the same reason.

I remember watching that television show *I Dream of Jeannie* when I was young, and I wondered how great it would be to have a Jeannie of my own, complete with the sexy outfit, who could blink a grilled-cheese sandwich out of thin air, all the while cleaning my room and doing my homework. I realize, of course, that is very silly and there is no such thing as a genie that lives in a lamp, but it makes me wonder if secretly we don't wish God were a genie who could deliver a few wishes here and there. And that makes me wonder if what we really want from the formulas are the wishes, not God. It makes me wonder if what we really want is control, not a relationship.

Some would say formulas are how we interact with God, that going through motions and jumping through hoops are how a person acts out his spirituality. This method of interaction, however, seems odd to me, because if I want to hang out with my friend Tuck, I don't stomp my foot three times, turn around, and say his name over and over like a mantra, lighting candles and getting myself in a certain mood. I just call him. In this way, formulas presuppose God is more a computer or a circus monkey than an intelligent Being. I realize that sounds harsh, but it is true.

I was watching *Booknotes* on CSPAN the other day and got caught up in an interview with a literary critic from the *New York Times.* The interviewer asked the critic why he thought the Harry Potter series was selling so many copies. "Wish fulfillment," the critic answered. He said the lead character in the book could wave a wand and make things happen, and this is one of the primary fantasies of the human heart. I think this is true. I call it "Clawing for Eden." But the Bible says Eden is gone, and as much as we want to believe we can fix our lives in about as many steps as it takes to make a peanut-butter sandwich, I don't believe we can.

So if the difference between Christian faith and all other forms of spirituality is that Christian faith offers a relational dynamic with God, why are we cloaking this relational dynamic in formulas? Are we jealous of the Mormons? And are the formulas getting us anywhere? Are modern forms of Christian spirituality producing better Christians than days long ago, when people didn't use formulas and understood, intrinsically, that God is a Being with a personality and a will of His own? Martin Luther didn't believe in formulas, and neither did John Calvin. Were they missing something, or are we?

After the writers' seminar, and after my friend told me reality was like fine wine, I started reading the Bible very differently. I stopped looking for the formulas and tried to understand what God was trying to say. When I did that, I realized the gospel of Jesus, I mean the essence of God's message to mankind, wasn't a bunch of hoops we needed to jump through to get saved, and it wasn't a series of ideas we had to agree with either; rather, it was an invitation, an invitation to know God.

I know there are people who have actually gone from misery to happiness, but they didn't do it by walking through three steps; they did it because they had a certain set of parents and heard a certain song and knew somebody who had a certain experience and saw some movie, read some book, had something happen to them like a car wreck or a trip to Seattle. Then they called on God, and a week later read something in a magazine or met a girl in Wichita, and when all this had happened they had an epiphany, and somebody may have helped them fulfill what this epiphany made them feel, and several years later they rationalized this mystic experience with three steps, then they told the three steps to us in a book. I'm not saying they weren't trying to be helpful; I bring this up only because life is complex, and the idea that you can break it down or fix it in a few steps is rather silly.

The truth is there are a million steps, and we don't even know what the steps are, and worse, at any given moment we may not be willing or even able to take them; and still worse, they are different for you and me and they are always changing. I have come to believe the sooner we find this truth beautiful, the sooner we will fall in love with the God who keeps shaking things up, keeps changing the path, keeps rocking the boat to test our faith in Him, teaching us to not rely on easy answers, bullet points, magic mantras, or genies in lamps, but rather rely on His guidance, His existence, His mercy, and *His love*.

Personally, I was miserable before I understood these ideas, but now I am so happy I laugh all the time, even in my sleep.

Sorry, I couldn't resist. On to Chapter Two!

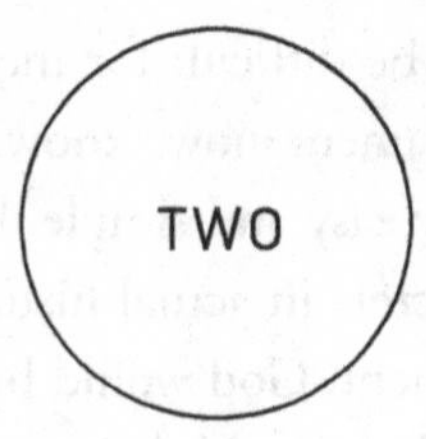

Impostors

Santa Takes a Leak

Relationships aren't the best thing, if you ask me. People can be quite untrustworthy, and the more you get to know them—by that I mean the more you let somebody know who you really are—the more it feels as though something is at stake. And that makes me nervous. It takes me a million years to get to know anybody pretty well, and even then the slightest thing will set me off. I feel it in my chest, this desire to dissociate. I don't mean to be a jerk about it, but that is how I am wired. I say this because it makes complete sense to me that we would rather have a formula religion than a relational religion. If I could, I probably would have formula friends because they would be safe.

I have this suspicion, however, that if we are going to get to know God, it is going to be a little more like getting to know a person than practicing voodoo. And I suppose that means we are going to have to get over this fear of intimacy, or whatever you want to call it, in order to have an ancient sort of faith, the same faith shared by all the dead apostles.

Jesus helps, to be sure, because He comes off as more or less trustworthy. If it weren't for Jesus, it would be difficult for me to follow God. When you read the Old Testament now, knowing exactly where the Book is going, it is all very easy and simple, but it wouldn't have been that way to the characters in actual history. If I had been around back in the Old Testament, God would have come off as more or less frightening. And I don't think I would have been able to know in my heart that it was the grandness of His nature, not the ease of His anger, that produced the fear.

My friend Penny's dad says he thinks God was angry for a while after the Fall, then got over it, sent His Son, and now is pretty well adjusted and forgiving. And of course I don't think that is exactly how it is, but I can understand why Penny's dad would read the Bible this way. But my other friend John MacMurray says that every time he gives the Bible to a person to read for the first time, even if they don't agree with it, they see God as a Person who is incredibly patient with humanity. John pointed out that it takes God hundreds of years to finally get angry enough to lay any sort of punishment on His enemies. He's like France in that way.

If the essence of our spirituality lies in a relationship with God, I suppose we should ask ourselves who God is. I would like to believe God is completely good, completely kind and forgiving, and it is we who aren't all that good and have no idea what goodness is in the first place. I realize that sounds like humanity-bashing, and I don't mean to bash humanity, but when I watch the news it makes me wish deep down for another time and place that has a king who is good, and a people who love and care about one another and are easy to trust, and a news channel that isn't always trying to stir up a fight so they can cover a fight. And Jesus helps me believe such a time and place might exist. I realize a lot of people don't like Jesus, or just ignore Him or have no use for Him, but I think the best thing a person can do is to read through the Gospels in the Bible and really look at Jesus, because if a person does this, they will realize that the Jesus they learned about in Sunday school or the Jesus they hear jokes about or the skinny, Gandhi Jesus that exists in their imaginations isn't anything like the real Jesus at all.

One of my roommates, Stacy, travels the world and shows *The Jesus Film*, a movie about the life of Christ, to people who don't have any idea about Jesus. Last summer Stacy led a group of African-American students to Africa where they showed the film to people on college campuses in Botswana. They were all sitting around one night watching this Jesus film, eating popcorn or whatever they do, when one of the American students came over to Stacy and asked why the guy in the film, the guy who played Jesus, was a white guy. Stacy thought about it for a second and then looked at the student and shrugged his shoulders. But it made Stacy wonder why the actor was a white guy because Jesus was Jewish and would probably have had an olive complexion and dark eyes and dark features.

Stacy, who is very kind and smart, gathered all the students on his team and asked them if the actor bothered them, and they talked about it for many hours. I would love to have been a fly on the wall because it seems to me we are all guilty of changing Jesus around in order to make Him more like ourselves. The guys on the team were very kind and gracious, and they loved the film because in the end they felt it didn't matter what color Jesus is, but that He loves them and invites them to love Him back. So they kept showing the film, and more than one thousand students who saw the film that summer believed in Jesus because they felt some quality they saw in His person and His character was the solution to something.

When I was a kid I used to listen to this Mark Cohn album over and over. He had a song on it about his father and how his father had a silver Thunderbird and used to get up in the morning, very early, and start the car and go driving down the street. Mark Cohn's father used to say that a Thunderbird is better than a Buick, and a Thunderbird is better than a foreign car, and if there is a God up in heaven, He drives a silver Thunderbird. I like that song, but I don't think God drives a silver Thunderbird. And I know nobody really believes that sort of thing, that God drives a Thunderbird, but there are people who believe other crazy ideas about God. I've met people who say God is mad at people, throwing dishes like an alcoholic on a binge, and others who paint God as a fairy running through flowers waving a wand at a unicorn. And all these people are convinced they are right.

The very scary thing about religion, to me, is that people actually believe God is who they think He is. By that I mean they have Him all figured out, mapped out, and as my pastor, Rick, says, "dissected and put into jars on a shelf." You've got a bunch of Catholics in Rome who think one way about God, and a bunch of Baptists in Texas who think another, and that isn't even the beginning. It goes on and on and on like this, and it makes me wonder if God created us in His image or if we created Him in ours. And it isn't just religion, either. I met a guy not long ago who was very conservative and had opinions all over him, and he was saying why God agreed with his political ideas and why that made his political ideas right. The whole time he was talking to me I was thinking about those guys in Africa, and I was feeling like this guy with the opinions was presenting a kind of Jesus who didn't even exist. His Jesus was just an invention of his imagination, someone who more or less justified his position concerning a lot of different political opinions. Sitting there listening to him made me feel tired. People like that should have an island.

But I suppose I can't blame him because, in my life, God is always changing the way I think of Him. I am not saying God Himself is changing, or that my theology is open and I blur the lines on truth; I am only saying I think I know who He is, then I figure out I don't know very much at all. For instance, and as I have said, a lot of people believe God responds to formulas, but He doesn't. So that is one example of how our idea of God is always becoming a bit more accurate. And that's one of the things you notice about Jesus in the Gospels, that He is always going around saying, *You have heard it said such and such, but I tell you some other thing.* If you happened to be a person who thought they knew everything about God, Jesus would have been completely annoying.

THE DEATH OF SANTA CLAUS

In my opinion, there are two essential problems with believing God is somebody He isn't. The first problem is that it wrecks your life, and the second is that it makes God look like an idiot.

When I was a kid and, to be absolutely honest, a teenager and perhaps even a young twenty-something, I believed God was like Santa Claus. I realize grown people should not think God is like Santa Claus, but you wouldn't believe how perfectly convenient it was for me to subscribe to the idea. The benefits were astounding. First: To interact with Santa Claus, I did not have to maintain any sort of intimate relationship. Santa simply slipped into the house, left presents, ate half a cookie, then hit the neighbors'. There was no getting us out of bed in the middle of the night to have sloppy conversations about why I was still wetting the bed.

Second: Santa theology was very black and white; you either made the list or you didn't and if you didn't, it was because you were bad, not because of societal pressures or biochemical distortions or your parents or cable television, but because you were bad. Simple indeed. Third: He brought presents based on behavior. If you were good, you got a lot of bank. There was a very clear reward system based on the most basic desires of the human heart: Big Wheels, Hot Wheels, Legos. You didn't have to get into the spirit of anything, and there was nothing sentimental that served as the *real* reason for the season. Everybody knew it was about the toys: cold, hard toys. Fourth: Kids who were bad got presents anyway.

Perfect.

Slowly, however, everything began to unravel. I tried to stop it because it was all so lovely and perfect, but there was nothing I could do. Truth grew in my mind like a fungus, and though I tried to keep it out, there was no resisting the epiphanies.

Santa went first, then God.

SANTA TAKES A LEAK

I remember being at the mall when I was eight and seeing Santa Claus relieve himself in the men's restroom. I was excited because we were going to see him that day, but I didn't want to disturb him, as he was hardly in his element. I watched him, though, his red suit, his white beard coming down his belly, his loud, echoing belch coming off the walls, his spread-legged stance and the way he looked straight up at the ceiling as he shook the dew off the lily, as they say. It was quite an honor to stand next to him and use the big urinal and act like it was nothing substantial to be standing next to him, as though I didn't even believe in him the way my friends Roy and Travis Massie no longer believed in him. I believed in him, though. I believed he showed up at our house on Christmas, and it didn't matter that we didn't have a chimney because he could come in through the front door, which is what he preferred because, as my mother told us, he had some lower back pain from always picking up after the ungrateful elves.

The Santa in the bathroom was a very tall man, younger than you would think, a bit depressed in the eyes and unshaven under his beard (if such a thing is possible). "Ho, ho, ho, kid," he said to me, zipping up his fluffy pants. I didn't say anything back. I just stood there and peed on my shoes. He looked at me, raised his eyebrows, shrugged his shoulders, and walked out.

That is when I realized the most terrible thing I'd ever realized: Santa doesn't wash his hands after he uses the bathroom. *How awful*, I thought to myself. And I was horrified. All those little bacteria, the little flus and colds and cancer bacteria that grow in small villages on a person's hands if he doesn't wash them. I could see in my mind the village of bacteria on Santa's hands; a kind of Tim Burton version of the microbial North Pole; all the textures and contours of the village correct, but the colors off; grays for greens, blacks for blues, lots of coughing, lots of mad cows.

I washed my hands and joined the family already in line. I watched as Santa's dirty hands grabbed kids to pick them up and set them on his knee. I watched as he patted their backs and, *heavens no*, their heads. It made me want to throw up, if you want to know the truth. I asked my mother if I could skip meeting Santa, and she told me I could go across the aisle to Ladies' Underwear and sit quietly on the floor, which is what I did, sitting there quietly on the floor, pointing women toward lingerie I thought might fit them best, trying to be helpful, trying not to think about the fact that Santa Claus of all people doesn't wash his hands.

That same year I learned Santa Claus actually had several clones, about seven or something, and they worked different department stores in the Houston area but magically became one on Christmas Eve. And I learned the next year that Santa didn't exist at all. I will never forget the day I found out because it was terrible. I was alone in the huge backseat of our Ford Grand Torino, and my mother and sister were in the front seat, and we were driving to my grandmother's house.

My mother had been acting very peculiar, asking us what we had heard at school and what did we think about Santa Claus and finally she just said it: She told my sister and me that Santa didn't exist, and my sister, who was two years older and had already dealt with the idea the previous year, leaned over the front seat to see if I was going to cry about it. I gripped the seatbelt very hard and clenched my teeth and sat up very straight like somebody taller and opened my eyes as wide as I could to keep them dry. My sister leaned in close, straight up to my nose, and I was trying my hardest not to blink when the moisture, suddenly and to my horror, drew to the corner of my right eye where it gathered to a certain mirth, collected in a puddle, then slid down my cheek like a penguin off a glacier. My sister exploded into laughter like she was watching a Jerry Lewis movie, slapping her knee and the whole bit. It took us another twenty minutes to get to my grandmother's house, and I sat in the backseat and tried not to make any noise. My sister would be very, very quiet until I let out a breath and a sob, and then she would explode into laughter again, slapping her knee and looking over at my mom, who was rolling her eyes.

I didn't stop crying for more than an hour. The loss of Santa was, at that time, the most dramatic loss of my young life. I could feel in the chill of the air the chasm, the fields of flat snow that blanketed the North Pole where once stood candy-cane villages, elves hammering at toys, warehouses filled with packages, upon one of which my name was written in the language of barcode. It was too much. I breathed and sobbed for more than an hour and calmed down only after I was assured we would still be receiving presents.

But after that it didn't take me very long to get over it, if you want to know the truth. In fact, if I remember correctly, I got a slight feeling of superiority by telling the other kids at school that he didn't exist. And after giving it some thought, having met Santa in the men's restroom, I can't say it troubled me to find out he was an impostor, that basically people just go around dressing up like Santa in order to fool the naive and make a little extra Christmas money.

IMPOSTORS

That is good and fine when we're talking about Santa, but when we're talking about God, the ramifications of an impostor are more upsetting. There are, after all, a lot of people who don't believe in God because they can't reconcile their idea of Him with the idea presented on television. By that I mean televangelists and conservative talking heads who confuse good-ol'-boy politics with Christian spirituality. And that is just the beginning.

Yesterday I watched the CSPAN coverage of the report issued by the independent committee that investigated the Catholic church, and they have discovered more than ten thousand cases of sexual misconduct by priests against children. This is a very sad thing because most of the Catholics I know are quite wonderful people who love one another, care about one another, and are involved in defending social justice. The whole scene reminds me of all the crap Jesus was up against, having to overcome the unkindness, unfairness, immorality, and injury done by squeaky-wheel religious leaders of the day.

And if you thought the Catholics were bad, you should take a look at us evangelicals. Occasionally, as I flip through television stations, I find a man named Robert Tilton, who, in the early 1990s, was accused on ABC's *Primetime Live* of abusing his pulpit by stealing money from those who followed his television ministry. I did a little research and discovered that his church in Dallas, once more than five thousand members strong, has dwindled to the less than two hundred still faithful who, every Sunday, sit scattered in the mammoth auditorium, much of which is now closed off by curtains to hide its emptiness. Tilton left Dallas the year following the scandal. His ex-wife confessed in divorce proceedings that the televangelist had to carry a disguise kit with him everywhere he went and spent at least 50 percent of his time wearing a fake mustache or a wig. I read an article that said even though Tilton wore a fake mustache and a wig, the couple would often be recognized walking into a restaurant or a store and be greeted with boos and obscene gestures. *He deserved it,* I thought while reading the article.

While pastoring in Dallas, Tilton built a complicated direct-mail system, capturing the names and addresses of those who called in for prayer. He would then contact them by mail and ask them to return a "widow's step of faith," which meant a lot of cash, and if they did this, God would give them financial security. *Primetime Live* found a dumpster full of the prayer requests, most of them not even taken out of the envelopes.

Robert Tilton is now relocated to Florida and still rakes in hundreds of thousands of dollars running a similar operation, this time with no congregation, only a few cameramen who probably stand around rolling their eyes all the time. His stage looks like the sort of setup kids would create for a school play about gladiators, complete with Roman pillars from behind which he steps out like Jay Leno, smiling at the audience, telling them their day has come, that God is going to make them rich.

I thought about Santa in the bathroom at the mall when I saw Robert Tilton on television because there are probably a lot of very oblivious and beautiful people who dismiss God because of guys like him, and that, to me, is a remarkable tragedy. But I don't dismiss God because of guys like Tilton; guys like Robert Tilton make me like Jesus more because the people Jesus had the least patience with were the people who said they represented God but didn't. And at first, when I watched Robert Tilton on his new television show, talking behind his desk and asking for money every few minutes, I got very angry, but then I started feeling very sorry for him because I can't imagine he actually believes in God at all. I can't imagine what sort of horrible things are going to happen to him when he dies, what sort of terror he is going to face and what sort of begging and manipulating he is going to try to get out of what God has in store for him and to what degree God is going to make him pay for what he is doing to people.

One night after I watched Robert Tilton on television, I went for a walk through the park. It was very cold, and I was feeling dirty because I had spent so much time watching this man talk half-truths about God so he could get some money. I kept thinking about what a sad world it is where stuff like that can happen to people, and I wondered if I had ever done that sort of thing. I knew I had never used God to get money, but you know what I mean. I had probably used Him to support my political opinions, and I had probably used Him to make some girl think I was godly because church girls like that sort of thing and, like I said, I was feeling very dirty about the whole situation. I wondered if there were any old ladies who couldn't pay their rent or get food because they gave all their cash to Robert Tilton, thinking God was going to help them get rich and pay their bills.

As I've already mentioned, it's a very sad world, and you don't have to go very far at all to find stories that make you feel dirty and miserable at the same time. The bad thing to do when you are thinking a lot of sad thoughts is to go walking through Laurelhurst Park at night, because the paths wind around trees and the lampposts dot the paths like giant candles, round the pond and up the hill on the back side where all the flowerbeds are. You get to feeling so completely alone when you walk through the park at night.

The real thing that made me sad that day was that God, who I think is quite good, was being misrepresented so terribly in the media. I realize it isn't popular to say such things, that as a Christian writer I should keep my mouth shut and kiss everybody's butt, but it is difficult to do so when there are so many media-savvy idiots pretending to represent Jesus. Just this morning I watched a fellow on his Christian show talk about what we should be doing in Iraq, how we should be starving out clerics and sending more troops to shoot more bullets and drop more bombs. He's a preacher, for crying out loud. Why doesn't he just tell people about Jesus?

If I weren't a Christian, and I kept seeing Christian leaders on television more concerned with money, fame, and power than with grace, love, and social justice, I wouldn't want to believe in God at all. I really wouldn't. The whole thing would make me want to walk away from religion altogether because, like I was saying about Santa Claus, their god must be an idiot to see the world in such a one-sided way. The god who cares so much about getting rich must not have treasures stored up in heaven, and the god so concerned about getting even must not have very much patience, and the god who cares so much about the West must really hate the rest of the world, and that doesn't sound like a very good god to me. The televangelist can have him for all I care.

You know, the real problem with God-impostors is that they worship a very small god, a god who exists simply to validate their identities. This god falls apart as soon as you touch him, as soon as you start asking very basic questions about the sanctity of all human life, the failure of combat mentality, and the lustful love of power.

When I was in high school, this simple god stopped making sense to me. I renounced my faith as soon as I stopped toeing the party line and started asking questions. Here's how my renouncing my faith went:

My senior year in high school I had taken a class on psychology and, as a last project, our teacher assigned each of us a prominent psychologist who had come up with what is called a personality theory, which essentially means an explanation for why people do everything. So for our last assignment, we were supposed to study and explain a personality theorist to the class in an oral presentation. There were all sorts of characters to choose from: Freud, as we know, was hung up about sleeping with his mother; and this other fellow named Skinner used to put his kid in a box and make her bark for cheese, or whatever he did; and then there was Pavlov, who drove his dogs crazy with bells and milkbones. I wanted to do my presentation on Skinner, and I was going to make up this whole story about how my uncle used to put me in a box and make me bark for cheese and that is why I had a twitch (I was going to have a twitch), but my classmate Brice Henderson got Skinner and I got this guy named Abraham Maslow, who, on account of the fact he was terminally boring and never dated, thought up a theory called the

"Hierarchy of Needs," which sounds much more exciting than it actually is, believe me.

Maslow held that man was motivated within a hierarchy of desires: A person would seek food, then shelter, then sex, then companionship, and on and on. Only when one need had been fulfilled would he pursue the next until, at last, he had achieved what he referred to as "self-actualization." I don't remember what Maslow said happens after self-actualization. I suppose a person wins a stuffed bear; the specifics of the theory escape me. And it was all good and fine and I had no problem with any of it, until . . .

One of the needs on Maslow's pyramid was the need to know God. Not to *know* God, but rather to supply for the human psyche a kind of divine heritage providing, among other benefits, an explanation for existence. Because science is severely deficient in details of origin, Maslow held that man had invented God as a kind of false bridge from one need to the next. God, far from a Being who had revealed Himself to man, was more an intellectual cuddly toy with which man snuggled during his dark night of the soul. God, in other words, was somebody who validated man's identity. Man needed God to shove into the crack created by the truth of his meaninglessness. Maslow would later recant this idea, but for me, the damage was done. And for the first time in my life, I had questions, and they weren't surface-level questions either; they were very deep, emotional questions. Maslow was describing the God I knew, the God of simple answers to simple questions, the God of *Keep your mouth shut and think what I tell you to think.*

I grew up hearing about God, hearing that He had created the universe, some animals, the Grand Canyon, that we weren't supposed to have sex or drink whiskey or go to dance clubs, that sort of thing, you know. *He's making a list, He's checking it twice, He's gonna find out who's naughty or nice. . . .*

Maslow's God, like the one I believed in, was a bridge for the psyche, an invention to calm our nerves and keep us in line. The small church I had been raised in, and from which my framework for God had been hoisted, provided no bulwark of protection from this attack, but rather an unfortified access to a straw man. We were all getting cuddly with Father Christmas, it seemed. I didn't have a relationship with God; I had a relationship with a system of simple ideas, certain prejudices, and a feeling that I and people who thought as I thought were right.

It took me three weeks of thinking to get up the nerve to tell God He didn't exist. At the time, I had a habit of taking walks in the middle of the night. I would leave the house around midnight and walk the streets till one or two in the morning. I don't do that sort of thing anymore, but back then, in my teens, it was the only time in my small, traffic-congested suburban town you could find some peace. I would walk down our street under a tunnel of oaks and pecans, up close to the highway and through the middle of the car wash, the pavement still wet with suds, the stoplight at Mikawa and 35 glistening green then yellow then red against the glossy pavement. Sometimes I would tie the trigger open on the car-wash wand, release the hose from the holster, drop a few coins in the slot, step away, and let the black snake snap in the air, up against the tin walls of the stall and back against the pavement.

I had been thinking about the whole Maslow thing for a few weeks, maybe a month, and I realized somewhere in this philosophy that provided an excuse; I could, if I wanted, walk away from God. I mean, if God didn't answer the serious questions about life, then I didn't have any responsibility to believe He existed. At first it was frightening, but I could feel in my heart that I wanted to dissociate, that if I walked away from God I would have a kind of freedom.

All this was happening during the times I would go walking at night. I would set the hose free while listening to music on my headphones; the Smiths made the hose snap around so beautifully you could get hypnotized by it, Kings X made it violent but purposeful and got you wanting to wreck something. The soundtrack to the movie *Glory* was the best, though, putting the whole thing together perfectly and almost explaining it to the emotions: the force of the water against the resistance of gravity. And when it was done the hose would go out slowly, like a snake losing air, lying there against the grate heaving and spitting. I realize this is all very melodramatic, but I was just out of high school and when you are that age, you don't realize you are just inventing drama for the sake of drama.

The night I told God He didn't exist I was watching the hose flail and listening to the Smiths sing "That Joke Isn't Funny Anymore," the endless echoing chorus of which rings out: *I've seen this happen in other people's lives, now it's happening in mine . . .*

When it was done the pavement turned from green to yellow, and I told myself when it turned red I would say it: I would tell God I no longer believed in Him, that I wanted to dissociate because He didn't explain anything, He was too simple and so He was a myth, a teddy bear; that Abraham Maslow was right and I would rather spend my life in dark truth than leaning against the crutch of feel-good propaganda about good people and bad people. The world was more complex than that and I knew it. I am not going to pretend this was an easy thing to do. It wasn't easy at all. Part of me wanted God to continue to exist. He had brought me a great deal of comfort and an identity and a community of friends who were quite kind and endearing and inclusive. My heart beat out blood and I could feel it thump so strongly I thought it was going to break my skin. The light turned red and I said it.

"You don't exist," I told Him.

Feet of Trees

What Do We Really Want?

I remember seeing that made-for-TV miniseries with Shirley MacLaine called *Out on a Limb.* There's a part in the movie where Shirley MacLaine goes for a walk on a beach and starts twirling around, saying, "I am God, I am God, I am God," right there in the waves. I heard a lecture by novelist Frank Peretti in which he wondered what that must have sounded like to God. He leaned up to the microphone and squeaked out, in a very little voice, "I am God, I am God." He got a big laugh out of that from the audience. What he was saying was that Shirley MacLaine's voice must have sounded very small to God, on account of she was standing way down on earth on a beach, twirling around.

I can understand why somebody would think they were God, though. In the first moments after I wake up, especially in the winter when I have left the windows open, I am quite taken aback by my existence; my hands, my eyelids, the feel of my feet rubbing against the blanket. In moments like this, I get the feeling that life is a great deal more complex than I am able to understand. I feel in these moments that I am fairly intricate and amazing;

a speaker for a mouth, two cameras for eyes, sticks for legs, a computer for a head, a million sensors in a million places. I could see how somebody would think they were a god; but I could also see how somebody would think that person was a nut too. If you are a god and I am a god, we are all gods and then the whole thing just gets boring.

I tell you all this only to say I came back to God. All the complexity about life was begging for an explanation; and me actually being god wasn't answering very many questions. And so in a way, I left the old god of easy answers, the god who was always wanting me to be rich or wanting my country to be better than other countries or, for that matter, for me to be better than you. I left that god the preachers talk about on television and the politicians mention in their prayers. But I left room open for another God, a God who might explain my existence, explain the complexity of my hands and feet and feelings and the very strange and mysterious fact that even as I type this I am breathing.

I confess, I feel there is a God who is very big and who understands everything. In the morning, when I get over these little moments of epiphany about how complex my construction is, I begin to *fear* the God that is, because He made all this that is our existence and He understands its physics. Whatever it is that understands the physics of this thing that is happening to us would have to be quite remarkable, with giant oaks for feet, perhaps, and a voice like wind through a forest and a mind that creates creations of which it might ponder in a way of learning what it already knows. I start to think about this and I confess, it stirs a certain fright and it helps me believe the Scripture that teaches *His ways are not like our ways.* (See Isaiah 55:8–9.)

I realize it isn't a big deal to fear God these days, but I do. By that I don't mean I have just a deep respect for Him or a healthy appreciation for Him; I actually get a general sense of terror. It isn't because I think He is a bad guy, because I don't. The sense of terror comes more from the idea that He is so incredibly other, has claimed He has created a kind of afterlife for people, has never been born and will never die and doesn't exactly live in a space. A God who is that different, that other, can tell you again and again He loves you and you are still going to be quite a bit afraid, just because of what it feels like when you think about His nature.

I say all this because the other side of what Shirley MacLaine was doing on that beach isn't funny. From God's perspective, looking down at this squeaky voice going off about how she is God is pretty funny, but the other side, the side that knows how very large God is, how He has no end, gives me a start something terrible. And I wonder what it sounded like to God when Jerry Falwell went on television and said the reason the twin towers were hit by those planes was because there were homosexuals in the building. I wonder what kind of annoying squeak that was in God's ear. I don't think a person who makes statements like that fears God. I don't think people like this respect God when He says to love your brother, love your enemy, turn the other cheek, don't judge lest you be judged, be patient, be kind, hold your tongue, and give every effort to keep the bonds of peace. Sometimes, honestly, I feel that squeaky-wheel Christian leadership can be as wrong about God as Shirley MacLaine. I don't think they actually fear Him or think He means what He says.

I was pleased to discover the God of Scripture is much larger than this. Everybody who met God in the Bible was afraid of Him. People were afraid of even the angels, so the angels always had to calm people down just to have a conversation. I would think that would be very annoying if you were an angel, always having to settle people down just to talk. It makes you wonder if the first thousand years in heaven will have us running around screaming like we would during an earthquake, the whole time God saying to us in an enormous, booming voice, *Calm down, calm down, will you, it's just Me.*

If you ask me, the way to tell if a person knows God for real, I mean knows the real God, is that they will fear Him. They wouldn't go around making absurd political assertions and drop God's name like an ace card, and they wouldn't be making absurd statements about how God wants you to be rich and how if you send in some money to the ministry God will bless you. And for that matter, they wouldn't be standing on a beach shouting about how they are God, twirling around in the waves. It seems like, if you really knew the God who understands the physics of our existence, you would operate a little more cautiously, a little more compassionately, a little less like you are the center of the universe.

One of the reasons I came to trust the God of the Bible was because He was big enough to explain the impostors. In Scripture, God never gets confused about who is and who isn't representing Him. Impostors represent a small god, a vapor in the imagination of a child, a god we would all do well to renounce.

The thing about the night at the car wash, the night I renounced my faith, was that I didn't think of God as being very big at all. The god I was renouncing was more an *idea* than a *person.* The god I used to know was a system of beliefs that made me feel right, not a living and active Being. That night, however, the idea-god fell away and the Person, the Being, the animate creature emerged in my mind. I walked back home after renouncing my faith. I walked through the oaks and the pecans, and I confess to you, I was scared. But I wasn't scared because God was there; I was scared because I felt like He wasn't. Don't get me wrong, I know the Bible says God will never leave us or forsake us, but when you go and tell Him to His face He doesn't exist, you run the risk of making Him angry. And even though I was losing the small god, in my mind I was renouncing God altogether, and I don't think this made God happy. Even though I used to take walks in the middle of the night, I had never been scared about it. People had thrown beer bottles at me and swerved at me in their cars, but I never got frightened. I always felt God was out there somewhere.

But that night it got pretty eerie as fingers from the oaks spread their thin stems in shadows across the road like cobwebs. I kept seeing what I thought were crouching men in alleys between houses, just there behind the trash can, just there in with the shrubs. I started walking very briskly, and even the sound of my feet came at me off house walls and wooden fences. I had never really thought about my life before, how it is kept up by breaths and spread atop time. My life suddenly seemed temporary, as though the expanse of it would be only eighty years, and if somebody took it from me now, I wouldn't get the little charity that was being thrown to me from nature, that is, the rest of my existence.

Before, my mind had me going out into eternity, the number of days making the individual nearly worthless in the whole, but now each moment had consequence. Cars in the distance stopped and pulled off the road for no reason, bugs in trees screamed out like cannibals, even cats padding gentle steps through porch-light made me nervous. And this pitted me against creation. Creation had a power it had not hitherto enjoyed. Creation could take my life; a man with a knife, hoodlums looking for trouble, drivers drunk at the wheel, cannibal bugs in trees, cats in porch-light.

I had become a chicken.

This wasn't something I expected. I thought when I told God He didn't exist, I would feel a sense of freedom. I thought my confessing that God didn't exist would relieve me from the responsibility of being one of His creations, but that isn't what it felt like; it felt more like I had been removed from His protection. I am not saying that is what actually happened, because who knows what actually happened; I am only saying that is what it felt like.

And then the odd thought occurred to me that I had *told* God He didn't exist. *I told Him.* What's the use in talking to a person to tell them they aren't there? As a child, after hearing the truth about Santa, I never had the desire to write him to tell him he didn't exist. I remember very well being quite upset about the idea, but never going on believing the man was real despite the report he wasn't. As a child, when I was told about Santa, it was as though a red thread had been pulled from a gray cloth, leaving a long chasm in the fabric; and then my mind was able to feel the chill the chasm had been letting in all along, the lack of mystery about Christmas, the lack of goodness in the world, the need for myth to smooth cracks in the mind. With God, however, it was as though a thread had been pulled from the fabric to reveal a thread of a different color, a color less me-pleasing, but a color all the same. God was still there. I tried to shake Him, but I couldn't find a place where He wasn't. This doesn't prove He actually exists, I realize, but a person is often driven by his sentiments, his logic trailing behind his emotions as a pariah.

The God Who Makes Sense of Life

I began to slowly realize that the God of the Bible, not the God of formulas and bullet points that some have turned the Bible into, but the God of the actual Bible, the old one before we learned to read it like a self-help book, had a great deal to say to me. What I mean by this is the God of the Bible, and for that matter the Bible itself, started making sense of my deepest emotions, quirks, and sense of brokenness. Once I separated the little god from the big God, and the little-god impostors from the true and loving servants of God, I began to pay more attention. This God became very beautiful to me, in fact. The things He said, the people He chose to speak through, and even the way He worded His message became quite meaningful. The God of the Bible, in a very strange way, even explained why I would have wanted to renounce my faith. Let me explain:

I've always been the kind of guy who likes to be seen as smart. It's not as bad as it sounds because I don't go around saying all kinds of smart-guy stuff to make other people feel like jerks or anything; it's just that I was never very good at much of anything else, you know, like I would try basketball for a while and when I was a kid I played soccer and tennis, but I was never very good at any of that, and then I learned to play the guitar but got very bored because what I really wanted was to be a rock star, not to actually play the guitar. So about the time I told God He didn't exist, I was desperate for an identity.

While this was taking place in my life I happened to attend a lecture by the chairman of the American Debate Team, who was about twenty-five or so, and there were a lot of girls in the audience because he was very rich and good-looking. The people at the school were going to videotape him talking about China or something, but the video camera was having trouble. The chairman of the American Debate Team had to stand on the stage for about twenty minutes with his hands in his pockets like an idiot, so what he did while he was standing there was recite poetry. I'm not making this up; this guy recited about a million poems, such as Kipling's *The Vampire* and parts of Longfellow's *The Song of Hiawatha.* He was very good at it and said the poems with the right spacing so it sounded like he was speaking beautiful spells, and all the girls in the audience were falling out of their chairs on account of their hearts were exploding in love for him. So then the people at the school got the camera working and the chairman of the American Debate Team gave his lecture about China, but the whole time I was sitting there I wasn't thinking about China; rather, I was wondering how I could get my hands on some poetry books and start memorizing them right away, on account of how much the girls liked it when the chairman of the American Debate Team recited poems. What I really began to wonder, I suppose, was whether or not coming off as a smart guy who knows poems could be my identity, could be the thing that made me stand out in life.

Now I didn't realize it at the time, but I would come back to this moment much later in life and realize something very important about myself, namely that I felt something missing inside myself, some bit of something that made me feel special or important or valued. This thing missing inside me, I realized, is something God would go to great lengths to explain in His Bible. This missing something was entirely relational, and by memorizing poetry, by trying to find an identity, and even by renouncing my faith at the car wash, I was displaying some of the very ideas God would speak of in Scripture, some of the ideas about being separated from a relationship that gave me meaning, and now looking for a kind of endorsement from a jury of my peers.

Here is how it all panned out: I had this friend Brian, who was a rugby player and who also was at the lecture, and afterward we were talking about China in the lobby when we looked over at the chairman of the American Debate Team with all sorts of girls around him, and that very day Brian and I decided we would start memorizing poems. By the next day we had Kipling's *The Gods of the Copybook Headings* memorized, which is a boring poem about being a conservative, and then I memorized *She Walks in Beauty* and *Had I This Cheek* and *The Tyger* and also *The Raven.*

Even though it's true that you can't memorize poetry and stay a fake, that sooner or later you start understanding what these poets are saying and it makes you feel life as something quite special with certain layers of meaning to it, at first you are doing it just to get people to think you are cultured. The thing about being smart about poetry that was different from being a guitar player or a tennis player was that I genuinely liked it and started feeling very good about myself because I had so much poetry memorized. I started reading a great deal and feeling very intelligent and would say little things that people would pick up on, and sooner or later I got this reputation as a smart and cultured person with *a reasonable amount of potential.*

I say all this because it is background information about what was really happening in my soul, the stuff the Bible goes to great lengths to explain. I figure I was attaching myself to a certain identity because it made me feel smart or, more honestly, it made other people tell me I was smart. This was how I earned my sense of importance. Now, as I was saying earlier, by doing things to get other people to value me, a couple of ideas became obvious, the first being that I was a human wired so other people told me who I was. This was very different from anything I had previously believed, including that you had to believe in yourself and all, and I still believe that is true, but I realized there was this other part of me, and it was a big part of me, that needed something outside myself to tell me who I was. And the thing that had been designed to tell me who I was, was gone. And so the second idea became obvious: I was very concerned with getting other people to say I was good or valuable or important because the thing that was supposed to make me feel this way was gone.

And it wasn't just me. I could see it in the people on television, I could see it in the people in the movies, I could see it in my friends and family, too. It seemed that every human being had this need for something outside himself to tell him who he was, and that whatever it was that did this was gone, and this, to me, served as a kind of personality theory. It explained why I wanted to be seen as smart, why religious people wanted so desperately to be right, why Shirley MacLaine wanted to be God, and just about everything else a human did.

Later, when I set this truth about myself, and for that matter about the human race, next to what the Bible was saying about who God is, what happened at the Fall, and the sort of message Jesus communicated to humanity, I realized Christian spirituality fit my soul like a key. It was quite beautiful, to be honest with you.

This God, and this spirituality, was very different from the self-help version of Christianity. The God of the Bible seemed to be brokenhearted over the separation in our relationship and downright obsessed with mending the tear.

I began to wonder if the actual language of life was not the charts and formulas and stuff we map out on a graph to feel smart or right, but rather the hidden language explaining why every person does everything they do, the hidden language we are speaking that is really about negotiating the feeling God used to give us.

I don't mean to sound like a pop psychologist. I am only pointing to the obvious stuff that is taking place in our souls that nobody wants to talk about. It is this obvious stuff that Scripture seems to waltz in and address matter-of-factly.

And that is the thing about life. You go walking along, thinking people are talking a language and exchanging ideas, but the whole time there is this deeper language people are really talking, and that language has nothing to do with ethics, fashion, or politics, but what it really has to do with is feeling important and valuable. What if the economy we are really dealing with in life, what if the language we are really speaking in life, what if what we really want in life is relational?

Now this changes things quite a bit, because if the gospel of Jesus is just some formula I obey in order to get taken off the naughty list and put on a nice list, then it doesn't meet the deep need of the human condition, it doesn't interact with the great desire of my soul, and it has nothing to do with the hidden (or rather, obvious) language we all are speaking. But if it is more, if it is a story about humanity falling away from the community that named it, and an attempt to bring humanity back to that community, and if it is more than a series of ideas, but rather speaks directly into this basic human need we are feeling, then the gospel of Jesus is the most relevant message in the history of mankind.

As I said before, the god I renounced that evening at the car wash was an impersonal god, a god of rules and lists and formulas. But what if all our rules and lists and formulas came together for a reason, and what if we stopped looking *at* the rules and lists and formulas and rather looked *through* them at the larger and more obvious message? What if the motive behind our theology was relational? My need, the brokenness that existed inside me and led me to play guitar and memorize poems and even renounce my faith in an effort to think myself smart, was all driven by relational motives: I wanted other people to value me. So what if the gospel of Jesus was a message that was relevant to that need?

I realized that. Jesus was always, and I mean always, talking about love, about people, about relationship, and He never once broke anything into steps or formulas. What if, because we were constantly trying to dissect His message, we were missing a blatant invitation? I began to wonder if becoming a Christian did not work more like falling in love than agreeing with a list of true principles. I had met a lot of people who agreed with all those true principles, and they were jerks, and a lot of other people who believed in those principles, but who also claimed to love Jesus, who were not jerks. It seems like something else has to take place in the heart for somebody to become a believer, for somebody to understand the gospel of Jesus. It began to seem like more than just a cerebral exercise. What if the gospel of Jesus was an invitation to know God?

Now I have to tell you, all of this frightened me a bit because I had always assumed a kind of anonymity with God. When I saw myself in heaven, I didn't imagine sitting at the right hand of God, as the Scripture says, but I pictured myself off behind some mountain range doing some fishing and writing a good detective novel. But if the gospel of Jesus is relational; that is, if our brokenness will be fixed, not by our understanding of theology, but by God telling us who we are, then this would require a kind of intimacy of which only heaven knows. Imagine, a Being with a mind as great as God's, with feet like trees and a voice like rushing wind, telling you that you are His cherished creation. It's kind of exciting if you think about it. Earthly love, I mean the stuff I was trying to get by sounding smart, is temporal and slight so that it has to be given again and again in order for us to feel any sense of security; but God's love, God's voice and presence, would instill our souls with such affirmation we would need nothing more and would cause us to love other people so much we would be willing to die for them. Perhaps this is what the apostles stumbled upon.

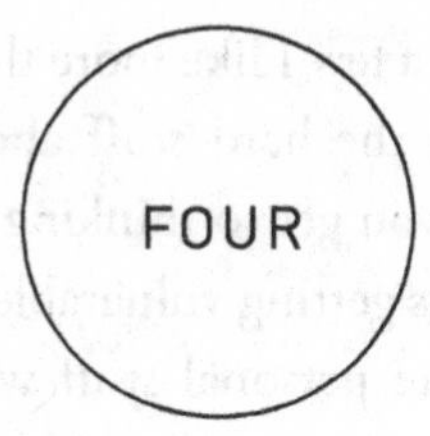

Free Verse

A Whole Message to a Whole Human Being

You would think some of the writers of the Bible would have gone to a Christian writers' seminar to learn the magical formulas about how to dangle a carrot in front of a rabbit, but they didn't. Instead, the writers of the Bible tell a lot of stories and account for a lot of history and write down a lot of poems and recite a great many boring numbers and then conclude with various creepy hallucinations that, in some mysterious way, explain the future, in which, apparently, we all slip into Dungeons and Dragons outfits and fight the giant frog people. I forget how it goes exactly, and I mean no disrespect. But because it is so scatterbrained, and has virtually no charts and graphs, I am actually quite surprised the Bible sells. Perhaps it's those lovely and colorful maps, which puzzles me because they aren't even current.

But I like the Bible. Now that I no longer see it as a self-help book, it has infinitely more merit. It has soul, I guess you could say.

As far as the writers in the Bible go, there are a few I like more than others. I like Paul the best because he said the hard stuff about women in ministry and homosexuality and you get to thinking he was pretty severe, and all of a sudden he starts getting vulnerable as though he is feeling lonely, needing to share personal stuff with somebody. When I come to these parts of his letters I feel he was writing late at night and was perhaps very tired, in some stranger's home who was intimidated because they knew his reputation but had only just met him. If you had a guy in your home who was always getting beat up about the faith, thrown in prison and that sort of thing, it would make you feel intimidated and nervous about having him in your home; it would make you wonder exactly how committed you are. I'll bet Paul didn't care, though; he doesn't seem like the type to judge people, but you know people were intimidated by him anyway.

He was terribly intelligent. For the first couple of days in a new town, Paul probably felt completely alone. I see him like this when he talks about how he wants to go home and be in heaven but stays on earth so he can write letters and preach. I see him writing by candlelight at a stranger's table when he talks about how he has this thorn in his flesh and can't get over it and prayed about it three times, but God said to him, "My grace is sufficient for you." It's writing like this that I like in a book. If a writer is going to sit down with a big important voice and try to get me motivated about something, I pretty much don't want to read anymore because it makes me feel tired, as though life were just about getting a lot of things done. Paul never did this. He was terribly personal.

The books I like are the ones that get you feeling like you are with a person, hanging out with a person who is being quite vulnerable, telling you all sorts of stuff that is personal. And that's the thing Paul did that makes me like him. The other thing is, the guy was passionate, like he actually believed this stuff was true, always going off about heaven and hell because he *knew* life has extremes. One minute he talked about how disgusting sin is and how it hurts God in His heart, and the next minute he said he would go to hell for people if he could, how he would die for them and go to hell if they would just trust Christ. It's really hard to read that stuff because it gets you feeling guilty about not loving people very much, and then you feel very thankful for people like Paul because it means that if a person knows Christ, they become the sort of man who says difficult truths with his mouth and yet feels things with his heart that make him want to go around and die for people. It's quite beautiful, really.

The next guy I like is John the Evangelist. That's what they called him back in the day. I like John because when he wrote his biographical essay about Jesus, he kept putting himself in the story; only he didn't call himself John, he called himself *the one whom Jesus loved.* You figure if a guy gets tortured and beat up and thrown in prison, he might start wondering whether God loves him anymore, but John didn't. And when John wrote his book he was always taking the camera to the outcasts, into the margins, showing how Jesus didn't demonstrate any favoritism. He showed how Jewish leaders ridiculed Christ, and he was fearless in exposing the hypocrisy of the ones who led with their heads, not their hearts. At the end of his essay, he captured an amazing conversation between Jesus and Peter. Jesus keeps saying to Peter, "Do you love Me?" And Peter keeps saying, "Yes, yes I do; You know that I do," but Jesus doesn't believe Peter and keeps asking him the same question again and again. It is quite dramatic, really.

The way John writes about Jesus makes you feel like the sum of our faith is a kind of constant dialogue with Jesus about whether or not we love Him. I grew up believing a Christian didn't have to love God or anybody else; he just had to believe some things and be willing to take a stand for the things he believed. John seemed to embrace the relational dynamic of our faith. And he did so in an honest tone, not putting a spin on anything. He revealed how none of the disciples truly understood Jesus and how they were all screwups, and he didn't make himself look good, either; he just told it exactly as it was. That's guts, if you ask me. And then, not unlike Paul, John closed his book with a lot of sentimental talk, very to the point but charged with meaning. He ended his book by telling the reader he was going to die. There were some people around back then who wondered if John was ever going to die because they had overheard Jesus say John would live forever, and because John got tortured and should have died early on, a lot of people assumed Jesus was saying John was going to live forever on earth.

This is beautiful and meaningful because John wrote his essay a long time after Christ had left so he was very old, probably nearly ninety years old, and this was back when communities loved old people. They didn't put them in homes to watch television; they gathered around them because they represented a kind of gentle beauty and wisdom. This was back when you didn't have to be all young and sexy just to be a person. And it makes you wonder if John sat and wrote that he was going to die knowing within a few days, a few weeks, a month of gentle good-byes, he was going to go home and leave all his friends, and he didn't want any of them to be surprised or scared.

When you read the book you start realizing that people who were very close to John read this essay and got to the end and started crying because John was telling them he was going to leave, and then I'll bet at his funeral everybody was standing around thinking about how John knew he was going to die and told them in his book. And I'll bet they sat around that night at somebody's house, and somebody who had a very good reading voice lit a candle, and they all lay on the floor and sat on pillows. The children sat quietly and the man with the voice read through the book, from beginning to end, and they thought together about Jesus as the man read John's book, and when it came to the end where John says he is going to die, the person who was reading got choked up and started to cry. Somebody else, maybe John's wife or one of his daughters, had to go over and read the end of it, and when she was finished they sat around for a long time and some of the people probably stayed the night so the house wouldn't feel empty. It makes you want to live in a community like that when you think about the way things were when Jesus had touched people.

A community like that might sound far-fetched, but when you read through John's other books, the short ones, all he talks about is *if you know Jesus, you will love your brother and sister*, and anybody who talked that much about loving your brother and sister was probably the most beloved person in their community, and when he died people would have felt a certain pain about it for a long, long time.

You don't have to read the Bible for long before you realize the folks who wrote this book were quite special, with enormous capacities for feeling and understanding truth. Paul and John are definitely my favorites, but after those two my favorite writer in the Bible is Moses. Moses maybe wrote the book of Job, and when he was finished he wrote Genesis through Deuteronomy.

I took a class on Moses from a man named John Sailhamer. It was the best class I have ever taken. I didn't normally take Bible classes back then, but my friend John MacMurray told me John Sailhamer is one of the smartest guys in the world when it comes to talking about Moses. I told him I still didn't want to go to the class, that I wanted to watch television, but at the time I was living with John MacMurray and his family, and he told me that I had to go if I wanted to continue living in his home. So I went to this class and about five minutes into it I knew I was taking the best class I would ever take. If you ever have the opportunity to take a class from John Sailhamer, you should. His knowledge concerning the Old Testament is quite ferocious.

At one point in the class, for instance, a lot of us were getting confused because we couldn't figure out what translation of the Bible he was teaching from, so we asked him. It turned out he was teaching from the ancient Hebrew, translating it in his mind into English as he went along. And you might think a guy like that would go around speaking Hebrew all the time to impress people but he didn't, except one time when he read a long piece of poetry that Moses wrote. He read it in Hebrew and it sounded so beautiful that when he was finished, even though none of us knew what he had said, we sat around very quietly because we knew we had heard something profound, something Moses had sat and labored over for a very long time, something that ancient Hebrews would have read and then stopped to slowly note the complexity of its beauty, and the depth of its meaning.

The thing about John Sailhamer is, he helped me love Moses. I don't know if I had given Moses much thought before that class, but after hearing John Sailhamer talk about him, he became a human being to me. Dr. Sailhamer said Moses, unlike most writers in Scripture, would stop the narrative to break into the kind of poetry he had quoted earlier, a kind of poetry called parallelism, which is when you say something and then repeat it using different phrasing. He said the way Moses wrote wasn't unlike the way people who write musicals stop the story every once in a while to break into song. At first I thought Dr. Sailhamer was just making things up, but he showed us in the text several places where the writer clearly stopped writing narrative and began writing poetry. The reason Moses would do this, according to John Sailhamer, is because there are emotions and situations and tensions that a human being feels in his life but can't explain. And poetry is a literary tool that has the power to give a person the feeling he isn't alone in those emotions, that, though there are no words to describe them, somebody understands.

I can't tell you how beautiful I thought this was; I had always suspected language was quite limited in its ability to communicate the intricate mysteries of truth. By that I mean if you have to describe loneliness or how beautiful your sweetheart is or the way a rainstorm smells in summer, you most likely have to use poetry because these things are not technical, they are more romantic, and yet they exist and we interact and exchange these commodities with one another in a kind of dance.

This comforted me because I had grown up thinking of my faith in a rather systematic fashion, as I said, listed on grids and charts, which is frustrating because I never, ever thought you could diagram truth, map it out on a grid, or break it down into a formula. I felt that truth was something living, complex, very large and dynamic and animated. Simple words, lists, or formulas could never describe truth or explain the complex nature of our reality.

What John Sailhamer was saying was meaningful because it meant God wasn't communicating to us through cold lists and dead formulas; it meant He wanted to say something to our hearts, like a real person. Remember when I was talking about a hidden language beneath the language we speak, and how this hidden language is about the heart? It seems the Bible is speaking this language, this inferred set of ideas, as much as it is speaking simple truths.

Furthermore, it is true God used a great deal of poetry in the Bible. David was a poet and his son Solomon created a musical called Song of Songs, which is about romance and sex, and even Paul had memorized the works of Greek poets so he could speak them from memory when giving a talk. If you quote a poem in a sermon today, some people think you are being mushy, but if you quoted one back in the day, people felt you were getting to the core of an idea, to the real, whole truth of it. And after taking John Sailhamer's class, I started wondering if the message God was communicating to mankind, this gospel of Jesus, was a message communicated to the heart as much as to the head; that is, if the methodology was as important as the message itself, that the ideas could not be presented accurately outside the emotion within which the truths were embedded.

And if you think about these things, it only makes sense that if God was communicating a relational message to humanity He would use the multilayered methodology of truth and art, because nobody engages another human being through lists and formulas. Our interaction with one another is so much more about that hidden language. I started wondering if our methodology, that of charts and formulas and lists, is not hindering the message Jesus intended. If our modern methodology is superior to the methodology of historical narrative mixed with music, drama, poetry, and prose, then why didn't God choose lists instead of art?

I began to wonder if the ancient Hebrews would have understood this intrinsically, if they would have sat around watching plays and reading poems knowing this is where real truth lies, and if our age, affected by the Renaissance and later by the Industrial Revolution, by Darwin and the worship of science, hasn't lost a certain understanding of truth that was more whole. If you have a girlfriend and you list some specifics about her on a piece of paper—her eye color, her hair color, how tall she is—and then give her this list over a candlelight dinner, I doubt it will make her swoon. But if you quote these ideas to her in a poem:

She walks in beauty like the night
Of cloudless climes and starry skies
And all that's best of dark and bright
Meet in her aspect and her eyes . . .

. . . she is more likely to understand the meaning, the value inferred by your taking notice of her features. The same ideas, expressed in poetry, contain a completely different meaning. She would understand you were captivated by a certain mystery in her aspect, in her eyes and her stride and the features perfectly met upon her face. And while our earlier conceived *list* of features might have been accurate, it certainly wouldn't have been meaningful.

It makes you wonder if guys like John the Evangelist and Paul and Moses wouldn't look at our systematic theology charts, our lists and mathematical formulas, and scratch their heads to say, *Well, it's technically true; it just isn't meaningful.*

If you ask me, the separation of truth from meaning is a dangerous game. I don't think memorizing ideas helps anybody unless they already understand the meaning inferred in the expression of those ideas. I think ideas have to sink very deeply into a person's soul, into their being, before they can effect change, and lists rarely sink deeply into a person's soul.

The difference between meaning and truth is quite simple, really. It is something we all understand and operate within daily. Several years ago, for instance, I chewed tobacco: long-cut Wintergreen Skoal. I know, I know, it was terrible for me. It causes cancer of the mouth and is bad for your heart and your breath, and girls are never going to want to kiss you if you chew that stuff. I knew all that for years and yet I couldn't kick the habit, mainly because I didn't want to. The tobacco gave me a little buzz and helped me relax. But I tried to stop. I went to Web sites and looked up statistics about the health risks of chewing tobacco. I printed the statistics and placed them on my desk where I could read them when I was tempted. But it didn't help. I still bought a can of the stuff every other time I gassed up my car. This went on for at least a year, until . . .

I was listening to the radio one afternoon, editing a chapter in a previous book, when a voice came on, very distorted and troubled. The man sounded as though part of his face were missing, low and muffled and slobbery. Between songs, the radio station had inserted a commercial, a public service message about the danger of using chewing tobacco. The man in the commercial said half his jaw had been removed, that he had no lower lip, and the reason his face was deformed was because for years he had used smokeless tobacco. He didn't list any facts, he didn't speak of any harmful ingredients, he didn't say he was going to die of cancer. And yet the image of a man without a chin speaking into the microphone was enough to convince me to stop. I never used the stuff again. I just didn't want to.

After taking John Sailhamer's class, I thought about my experience with chewing tobacco in connection with understanding the difference between meaning and truth. I wondered if when we take Christian theology out of the context of its narrative, when we ignore the poetry in which it is presented, when we turn it into formulas to help us achieve the American dream, we lose its *meaning* entirely, and the ideas become fodder for the head but have no impact on the way we live our lives or think about God. This is, perhaps, why people are so hostile toward religion.

While having dinner with a friend recently, she commented that the primary concern for Christians today is to translate the precepts of Scripture for a postmodern audience. And I don't know what *postmodern* means, but I kindly disagreed with her and wondered out loud if we didn't need to stop translating the Bible for a modern audience, an audience endeared to the simplification of reality, an audience that likes to memorize lists in an attempt to understand God. Perhaps if we stop reducing the text to formulas for personal growth, we can read it as stories of imperfect humans having relations with a perfect God and come to understand the obvious message He is communicating to mankind.

I was reading *The Cloister Walk* by Kathleen Norris the other day, and she was talking about Benedictine monks and how they would sit up late at night to study the Bible by candlelight. I wondered what it would have been like to study the Bible and not be tainted by lists and charts and formulas that cause you to look for ideas and infer notions that may or may not be in the text, all the while ignoring the poetry, the blood and pain of the narrative, and the depth of emotion with which God communicates His truth. I think there would be something quite beautiful about reading the Bible this way, to be honest—late at night, feeling through the words, sorting through the grit and beauty. It wouldn't bother me at all to read the Bible without the charts and lists because a person could read the Bible, not to become smart, but rather to feel that they are not alone, that somebody understands them and loves them enough to speak to them—on purpose—in a way that makes a person feel human.

Here is what Kathleen Norris said about those monks:

> Although their access to scholarly tools was primitive compared to what is available in our day, their method of biblical interpretation was in some ways more sophisticated and certainly more psychologically astute, in that they were better able to fathom the complex, integrative, and transformative qualities of revelation. Their approach was far less narcissistic than our own tends to be, in that their goal when reading scripture was to see Christ in every verse, and not a mirror image of themselves.

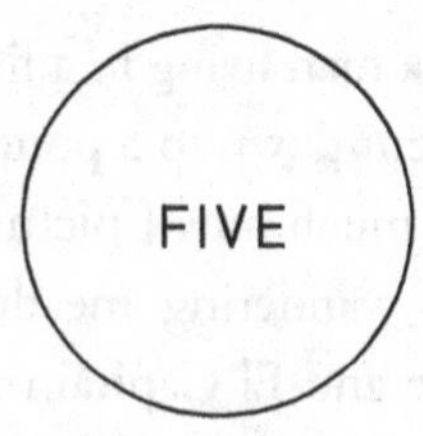

Naked

Why Nudity Is the Point

About the time I took John Sailhamer's class, I took a trip to Yosemite. Every two years or so I go to Yosemite because, in my opinion, Yosemite Valley is the most beautiful place in all America. If you don't get to a beautiful place every couple of years, you get to thinking everything is urban, as though when God made creation He just made some medium-size buildings, a bowling alley, and a burger place. The thing is, the last time I was in Yosemite Valley, I was thinking about the Garden of Eden.

Moses wrote about the Garden of Eden at the beginning of Genesis and because of John Sailhamer's class, I wasn't looking for a formula in the text, a few steps to make my life better; instead, I was reading it like literature, as though a human being were trying to tell me something about life, something he thought was beautiful or ugly, true or inspiring—you know the drill. And because I was reading the text this way, and because I was at Yosemite, I started realizing the Garden of Eden wasn't anything like I'd imagined. In the first place, the Garden was much larger than the territory I had pictured in my mind. Previously, when I thought about the Garden of Eden I pictured a woman and a man living in a little cottage with a trail outside their door that went down to a pond. I realize this is quite simple, but that is pretty much how I pictured it. Being in Yosemite, however, with that wandering meadow, Yosemite Falls feeding the green, Half Dome and El Capitain rising out of the earth more than two thousand feet, I realized the Adam I read about in Moses' book was a naturalist in an expanse perhaps as large as a continent.

Moses said a great river flowed out of the Garden, dividing into four rivers. The Pishon flowed through Gavilah, a land containing a great deal of gold and resin and onyx stone, whatever that stuff is; then the river split off into the Gihon and flowed through a land called Cush. And there were still two more rivers, the Hiddekel and the Euphrates. It is true that the great river, the river that created the other four, flowed *out* of the Garden of Eden, but for such a river to gather enough strength within the Garden to be split into four, defining the landscape for four territories, means the land that created the river must have been mammoth. This, of course, ended my thought of a little cottage, a path, and a pond.

And then I began to wonder about Eve, what the scene might have looked like when she and Adam first met. Milton paints the meeting as being more realistic than I had imagined, writing that the slow-to-love Eve did not find Adam the least bit attractive, becoming enamored, instead, with her own reflection in some water. It's true women are terribly enamored with their own reflections. You can't blame them, though. If I were good-looking, I would certainly go around looking at myself all the time, too. And it is also true women are slow to love. I used to think it was because something was wrong with them, but, over time, I wondered whether they were more deliberate than men about important decisions. Romantic decisions. And in comparison I realized they were infinitely more intelligent about relational matters than men.

But when I was reading the text the way John Sailhamer said to read the text, I noticed Adam and Eve didn't meet right away. Moses said God knew Adam was lonely or incomplete or however you want to say it, but God did not create Eve directly after He stated Adam was lonely. This struck me as funny because a lot of times when I think about life before the Fall, I don't think of people going around lonely. But that thought also comforted me because I realized loneliness in my own life doesn't mean I am a complete screwup, rather that God made me this way. You always picture the perfect human being as somebody who doesn't need anybody, like a guy on a horse out in Colorado or whatever. But here is Adam, the only perfect guy in the world, and he is going around wanting to be with somebody else, needing another person to fulfill a certain emptiness in his life. And as I said, when God saw this, He did not create Eve right away. He did not give Adam what he needed immediately. He waited. He told Adam to name the animals.

Now I had read this a thousand times, just glancing over it, you know, but this time, reading it without looking for a magical formula, I actually thought about what would be involved in a job as big as naming the animals. In my mind this had been such an effortless action; Adam sits on a log with his hand on his chin, God parades the animals by rather quickly, Adam calls out names under his breath: *Buffalo, chimp, horse, mouse, lizard, buffalo . . . Uh, wait—did I already say buffalo? Um, well—how about cow; did I already say cow?*

But could it really have been so effortless? On that particular trip to Yosemite I took along the journals of John Muir, the guy who came up with the glacier theory for Yosemite Valley, a theory that says great glaciers carved the rocks that make up the walls of the place. I sat there in Yosemite reading about Muir's glacier theory, knowing it took him years of research, experiments, and canvassing the valley to develop the philosophy, and I wondered in my mind how he must have sat on the mountainside, drawing diagrams of El Capitain and Half Dome, wondering about the great wall of ice that cut through the granite slopes. And if it took John Muir the better portion of his life to realize his theory about the landscape in small Yosemite, I wondered, then, how much longer it must have taken Adam to name the animals in all the earth. I wondered how long it must have taken him to journey to the ocean to name the sea life, and whether he had to make a boat and go out on a boat or whether God had them swim up close to the shore, so Adam only had to go in about waist-deep.

I looked up how many animals there are in the world, and it turns out there are between ten million and one hundred million different species. So even if you believe in evolution, that means there were between one million and fifty million species around in the time of the Garden, and Adam, apparently, had to name all of them. And the entire time he was lonely.

I never thought of Adam the same again. The image of the man holding the fig leaf over his privates seemed nearly crude. Rather this was a man who, despite feeling a certain need for a companion, performed what must have been nearly one hundred years of work, naming and perhaps even categorizing the animals. It would have taken him nearly a year just to name the species of snakes alone. Moses said that Eve didn't give birth to their third child till Adam was well into his hundreds, which means they would have had Cain and Abel some thirty or so years before, which also means either it took Adam more than a hundred years to name the animals, or he and Eve didn't have sex for a good, long, boring century. And so in my mind, I began to see Adam as a lonely naturalist, a sort of Charles Darwin character, capturing animals and studying their hooves and heads and tails and eating habits and mating rituals. It must have been absolutely thrilling work, to be honest, thrilling and more than a little tiring.

The thing is, when Adam finished naming the animals, after all his work and effort, God put him to sleep, took a rib out of his side, and fashioned a woman. I had read that part a thousand times, too, but I don't think I quite realized how beautiful this moment was. Moses said the whole time Adam was naming the animals, that entire hundred years, he couldn't find a helpmate suitable for him. That means while he was naming cattle he was lonely because he couldn't really communicate in the same way with the cattle, and when he was naming fish he probably wanted to go swim in the ocean with them, but he couldn't breathe underwater; and the entire time he could not imagine what a helpmate might look like, how a helpmate might talk, the ways in which a helpmate might think. The idea of another person had, perhaps, never entered Adam's mind. Just like a kid who grows up without a father has no idea what having a father would be like, a guy who grows up the only human would have no idea what having another human around would be like. So here was this guy who was intensely relational, needing other people, and in order to cause him to appreciate the gift of companionship, God had him hang out with chimps for a hundred years. It's quite beautiful, really. God directed Adam's steps so that when He created Eve, Adam would have the utmost appreciation, respect, and gratitude.

I think it was smart of God because today, now that there are women all around and a guy can go on the Internet and see them naked anytime he wants, the whole species has been devalued. If I were a girl today in America, I would be a feminist for sure. I read recently where one out of every four women, by the time they reach thirty, are sexually harassed, molested, or raped. And then I thought how very beautiful it was that God made Adam work for so long because there is no way, after a hundred years of being alone, looking for somebody whom you could connect with in your soul, that you would take advantage of a woman once you met one. She would be the most precious creation in all the world, and you would probably wake up every morning and look at her and wonder at her beauty, or the gentle, silent way she sleeps. It stands to reason if Byron, Keats, and Shelley made beauty from reflecting on their muses, having grown up around women all their lives, that even these sonnets could not capture the sensation Adam must have felt when he opened his eyes to find Eve.

You probably think I am being mushy and romantic, but the first time Moses breaks into poetry in the Bible is when Adam first meets Eve. The thing about Moses was, he was the king of understatements. He could pack a million thoughts and emotions into just a few words. Here's what he said about what Adam thought when he met Eve:

> *Bone of my bones*
> *And flesh of my flesh* (Genesis 2:23 NKJV)

If you think about these ideas they are quite meaningful, and the bit of poetry Moses came up with truly summarizes the scene because, for the first time in his life, Adam was seeing a person who was like him, only more beautiful, and smarter in the ways of love and encouragement, and more deliberate in the ways of relationships. He must have thought to himself that she was perfect, and after a few days of just talking and getting to know each other, they must have fallen deeply in love. After Adam had taken Eve to the distant mountains where they could look down on the four rivers, and after he built for her a home and showed her the waterfalls and taught her the names of all the animals, he must have gone on a long walk with God and thanked Him, and I'll bet that was a very beautiful conversation. I'll bet Adam felt loved by God, like he was somebody God was always trying to bless and surprise with amazing experiences, and I'll bet they talked together about how beautiful Eve was and how wonderful it was that the two of them could know her, and I would imagine that Eve felt safe, loved, not used or gawked at, but appreciated and admired.

I know it sounds sensational, but I used to think that story was just a cartoon, just some cutout figures on a felt board. But they weren't that at all; they were people, human beings, and they felt all the things we might expect them to feel. And certainly a lot of this stuff really did happen to them, and certainly Adam was taken aback by Eve, surprised and amazed, and this is summed up wonderfully in Moses' poem.

Considering this couple, and what Adam went through to appreciate Eve to the utmost, I wondered at how beautiful it is that you and I were created to need each other. The romantic need is just the beginning, because we need our families and we need our friends. In this way, we are made in God's image. Certainly God does not need people in the way you and I do, but He feels a joy at being loved, and He feels a joy at delivering love. It is a striking thought to realize that, in paradise, a human is incomplete without a host of other people. We are relational indeed. And this book, the Bible, with all its understanding of the relational needs of humans, was becoming more meaningful to me as I turned the pages. God made me, He knows me, He understands me, and He wants community.

I hiked around Yosemite Valley all day and wondered what it

would have been like to have the kind of relationship with God that Adam enjoyed. Adam and Eve, after all, are the only people in all of history who had a good relationship with God. Everybody else, after the Fall, had a pretty screwed-up idea of who God is, but Adam and Eve had the whole Deity before their eyes. And even though Adam was still lonely for a companion, I'll bet he didn't have any self-doubt or any low self-esteem because he had God there and, as I have said, just as a plant gets its life from the sun, people must have received their life from God. Jesus was always talking about how His glory came from God, as though God was shining on Him. The thing that made Jesus good, and the thing that made Adam good, was God's shining on them.

Can you imagine something like that, what it must feel like in the soul to have God's glory shining through you? With that much glory, that much of God shining through you, you would never have a self-defeating or other-person-bashing thought again. It would be brilliant. To say nothing of the earth, how wonderful it must have been, and to have had this wonderful woman Eve counseling you through the ways of love and relationships, but to have God shining through you is an idea, a mentality hardly imaginable. I'll bet I wouldn't think about any of the stuff I think about if I had God always shining life into my soul. I can hardly wrap my mind around the idea.

Do you know how Moses described the main characteristic of a person before the Fall? Moses said people before the Fall were naked and weren't ashamed. I'm not making this up. When he got to the end of chapter 2 of Genesis, the part of the Bible where he described what paradise was like, he concluded his description of paradise by saying Adam and Eve were *naked and were not ashamed.* It's right there in the Bible; you can look it up if you want. (See Genesis 2:25.)

Why Nudity Is the Point

Sitting there in Yosemite thinking about Adam and Eve being naked made me wonder if I would be comfortable in the Garden. In the first place, I hate being naked. The only time I get naked is when I am in the shower. Other than that I wear clothes all the time. And if I could wear clothes in the shower, I would. Here's the thing about being naked: When you're naked, all you're thinking about is the fact you're naked. If you go to the grocery store to get some barbecue sauce and you don't have on any clothes, chances are you aren't going to stand around looking for the barbecue sauce that's on sale, you're just going to grab the first bottle and get out of there on account of the fact you're naked. You aren't going to get a price check or go look to see if they have a new flavor of ice cream.

I know that sounds funny, but if you were to walk into the Garden of Eden, you would probably freak out Adam and Eve because they would think you had colorful skin made of cotton and they wouldn't have any idea that you were really a human with clothes on because, like Moses said, they were naked and weren't ashamed. The idea of clothes had never crossed their minds. And I know you think I am being immature by bringing this up, but the thing is, Moses repeated this idea five times. In just one hundred words used to describe Paradise and the Fall, the main thing he said, again and again, was that they were naked.

I wondered why it was that when people talked about the fall of man, about the Garden of Eden, they never talked about how people went around naked. If you ask me, the most obvious thing that happened after the Fall was that people started wearing all kinds of clothes. Just go to the store and look around, and you will see people wearing clothes. Everywhere you go you see people wearing clothes. Even as I type these words I am wearing clothes. I mean, evolution may explain how we came from apes, but it does nothing to explain why we wear clothes. And if Moses said it five times then you would think, when we consider the Garden of Eden and the fall of man, the first thing we would think of was that this was when we started wearing clothes. After all, it is the point of the story. Moses doesn't have any other point than this.

I started asking myself why Moses would say five times that people were naked before the Fall, but after the Fall, they went around with clothes on. So I read chapter 2 of Genesis again and, like I said, it was all about how nice Paradise was, and he summed up the description by saying Adam and Eve went around naked. Then I read chapter 3 and noticed something quite fascinating: The very first thing that happened after Adam and Eve ate from the Tree of Knowledge of Good and Evil was that they noticed they were naked. And man, I couldn't stop thinking about it; I couldn't stop thinking about how whatever happened at the Fall made them aware they were naked. This isn't "hidden wisdom" in the text. It is the text. It is blatant, and yet I had never heard anybody unpack it before.

And then it all came together. It all became so obvious, it was actually frightening. Moses was explaining all of humanity, right there in Genesis chapter 3, and because people were always reading it looking for the formula, they never saw it.

Here is what I think Moses was saying: Man is wired so he gets his glory (his security, his understanding of value, his feeling of purpose, his feeling of rightness with his Maker, his security for eternity) from God, and this relationship is so strong, and God's love is so pure, that Adam and Eve felt no insecurity at all, so much so that they walked around naked and didn't even realize they were naked. But when that relationship was broken, they knew it instantly. All of their glory, the glory that came from God, was gone. It wouldn't be unlike being in love and having somebody love you and then all of a sudden that person is gone, like being a kid lost in the store. All of the insecurity rises the instant you realize you are alone. No insecurity was felt when the person who loved you was around, but in his absence, it instantly comes to the surface. In this way, Adam and Eve were naked and weren't ashamed when God was around, but the second the relationship was broken, they realized it and were ashamed. And that is just the beginning.

If man was wired so that something outside himself told him who he was, and if God's presence was giving him a feeling of fulfillment, then when that relationship was broken, man would be pining for other people to tell him that he was good, right, okay with the world, and eternally secure. As I wrote earlier, we all compare ourselves to others, and none of our emotions—like jealousy and envy and lust—could exist unless man was wired so that somebody else told him who he was, and that somebody else was gone.

Think about it for a second. Moses, in chapters 2 and 3 of Genesis, has presented a personality theory more comprehensive than the writings of Freud, Maslow, Frankl, and Skinner combined. And he did it in only a hundred words.

Some scholars say that later in the text, when God sews clothes for Adam and Eve, Moses was saying God killed an animal, a sacrifice from which the clothes are sewn, and this acts as a kind of prophecy for the fact that much later man will be clothed in righteousness through Christ, the perfect sacrifice. I think that explanation is interesting, and it certainly fits in with our Christian theology, but in my opinion that isn't what Moses was saying.

The Bible is a relational document, and theology is basically the charts and lists we have made out of the document. It is great stuff to keep us in line, but in this case it may have caused us to miss a message powerfully relevant to mankind. It really is very simple, and yet when unpacked, serves as a miraculous account of the development of human personality. Moses was speaking very plainly and artfully, and in so doing he explained everything.

I used to think that when the Fall happened, man started lusting, getting angry, getting jealous, coveting, stealing, lying, and cheating because, in the absence of God, he became a bad person. And in a simple, children's-story sort of way this is true, but in Genesis 2 and 3, Moses explains exactly why all of us feel, act, desire, and dream the things we feel, act, desire, and dream. The ramifications of this obvious idea are nearly infinite.

Of course I am being technical about things. The truth is these were people. Adam and Eve were people. As I read Moses' account, and as I walked around Yosemite, I was rather endeared to them. I have wonderful friends in Canada named Kaj and Libby Ballentyne. Kaj and Libby started an outdoor Bible college many years ago, and they are constantly climbing mountains of ice or running rapids with students. They love nature and they love the God who seemed to make nature for them. They love each other and enjoy each other, and when they are apart for longer than a few days you can see it in their eyes how much they miss and need their friend.

I stood on a rock at Glacier Point and I imagined Kaj and Libby having the run of the Garden of Eden, hiking up into its steeps to catch a view of one of God's sunsets. And then it hit me how awful it must have been for Adam and Eve to have been deceived by Satan, to have been tricked into breaking their relationship with God.

You and I almost have it easier. We were born this way. But I remember loving a girl back in Colorado and having her explain to me she didn't feel the same and how for a year I lived in the attic of an old house in Portland, feeling an ache and emptiness in my heart I thought would never mend, sitting beneath a single dangling bulb reading Nietzsche. And this feeling, this feeling must have been so much more painful for Adam and Eve, this feeling of having an infinite amount of love pouring through their lives and then it's suddenly gone. I pictured my beautiful friends Kaj and Libby having to go through that kind of pain and it was almost too much. I wondered at how terrible it must have felt, at the fear of no longer feeling God, at the ache of emptiness and the sudden and horrifying awareness of self. God have mercy.

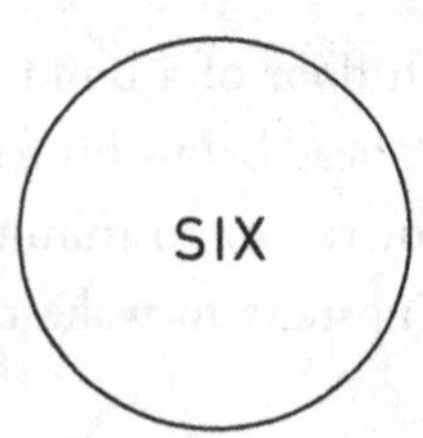

Children of Chernobyl

Why Did God Leave?

I was living at Graceland, the house on the traffic circle at Thirty-ninth and Glisan, when Tony the Beat Poet knocked loudly on the French doors that opened into my room. It must have been six in the morning and I confess, I was somewhat frustrated that I was being made to get out of bed that early. Back then I was working on a book and wrote mostly at night, so I hadn't gotten to bed till well after midnight the previous evening. I was groggy when I answered the door.

"Have you heard?" Tony asked in a panic.

"What are you talking about?" I said.

"Have you heard?" Tony said again, brushing past me into the house.

Tony looked terrible and anxious; the expression on his face, his tone—he wanted the television. He walked across the living room and turned it on, then backed himself to the couch slowly, sitting on the edge of it with his hand over his mouth. He had heard the news on his car radio and wanted to see the images. I sat down in the big brown chair and when my eyes focused I saw on

the screen a man jumping from the seventieth floor of a building in New York, his speck of body descending, his head below his feet, his tie flagging out behind him. I watched for ten or so minutes until the second tower collapsed, then went upstairs to wake the other guys in the house.

I remember going door-to-door at Reed College a few weeks after the terrorist attacks. It was the night all the freshmen were cramming for their first humanities paper, so we were delivering cookies, wishing them the best and giving them a break from their books. Reed is a liberal school, to be sure, and I suppose I was surprised at the patriotic sentiments pasted as cut-out editorials on dorm-room doors—the American flags, the pictures of the New York skyline. But I was walking a hall in the old dorm block sometime after midnight when I came across a door that had some anti-American reactions pasted as bumper stickers and taped-up notes, and next to these was a list of statistics regarding tragedies in the Middle East. Thousands are killed there every year, the statistics revealed, and to the people living there, losing three thousand people in one day is not a significant event. Death, in Gaza, in the West Bank, in Afghanistan, Pakistan, Iraq, and Iran is a way of life. I wondered at the complexity of the situation.

It was a somber time for all of us. Truth got lost in emotion, both for and against the West. I found myself sentimental at first, thinking of the firefighters going into the buildings, and then I found myself feeling for Arabs here in the States and abroad. I lost sentimentality about the time country-and-western singers came out of the woodwork to sing twangy and horribly written songs about why America is better than everybody else. It killed me. None of it was true. Then I got sad about it.

My friend Andrew the Protester had been on a bus in Portland, and he sat next to a man who happened to be Indian. This man who was from India was confronted and scorned publicly by another guy on the bus. The other guy told him he should be ashamed of himself and that he should go back home. He was Indian, for crying out loud. You wouldn't think a thing like that would happen here in Portland, but it does. A very close friend of mine, a very conservative missionary, told me he thought we should "bomb the rag-heads." And that is what we did a few months later in two separate campaigns. We bombed these countries, according to the president, because "they hated freedom."

I prayed a great deal during this time. We sat around in the lounges at Reed and watched the talking heads on television, we talked with students, we went to rallies, we protested acts of violence to end acts of violence, we listened to lectures, we read books, we watched more television. In a way it was odd directly after September 11 because it was as though everybody were taking a break from normal life, as though everybody were taking time off to attend a kind of national funeral. We all were quiet at first, all unified, but soon the reverence turned to opinions, and opinions to arguments, and arguments to rage.

We ached at the simplicity of proposed solutions. The spin. I remember feeling hopeless at the death of truth and seeing truth as this whispering weakling in the corner, a wallflower, having no say in the global conversation, having no guts to step forth and negotiate peace. I got sick of the emotionalism, the feelings that replaced the thoughts. "These colors don't run," a bumper sticker read. "Support our troops," a politician told us. All of it aimed at stirring up emotion rather than logic. We were living on sentimental clichés. Our country had become a team and we were wrapped up in whether or not we were going to win the *game* against *them.* It was like the World Cup, except with guns. They changed the name of French fries in the capital to freedom fries. I was embarrassed. The French are already so snobby to begin with, did we have to give them reason?

I hate war, to be honest. I hate *one side against another.* I hate groupthink. And war isn't new, either. It goes way back, all this tragedy. I remember when I was a kid, buying U2's new album *The Unforgettable Fire,* which was inspired by pictures captured after a plane called *Enola Gay* dropped a bomb called *Little Boy* on Hiroshima, Japan, an event that ended World War II. In Hiroshima, 70,000 people were killed instantly, and another 40,000 three days later in Nagasaki; another 110,000 were injured in the blasts, and another 340,000 died from diseases such as leukemia, all attributed to the nuclear fallout from the mushroom cloud. And the entire city of Tokyo was burned to the ground only weeks before these killings took place.

Last week I watched the Academy Award–winning documentary *Fog of War* about Robert MacNamara. In the movie MacNamara sat fidgeting in a chair and admitted our policies in World War II, and again in Vietnam, were less than honorable. And I know people who were in Vietnam, and I think they are heroes all the same, but it was so nice to sit in a movie theater and watch an eighty-year-old power broker admit he was wrong, that our reactions, that getting into the heat of battle had caused certain lapses in reason, understanding, and compassion. Hearing Robert MacNamara admit these things made me feel there was truth out there, that there was some kind of hope in humility, a humility that, perhaps, comes upon you just before you die, during that stage of life when you realize, for the first time, the *our team is better than your team* mentality will always fail.

I pulled out that U2 album I was talking about earlier. I put on a pot of coffee and listened to it in the morning before my roommates woke up. I listened to it as the sun came up over Laurelhurst, my windows open, the clouds coming in off the Pacific, stretching like wispy cobwebs into the blue, out toward the mountains. And the somber, reflective music seemed to re-create the devastation of World War II in my mind. I could see the bombs drop, the sudden deaths of thousands, those on the fringes running from the flames. I kept seeing the images they showed in that movie about Robert MacNamara, the images of Tokyo on fire, of the burned children screaming in Hiroshima and Nagasaki. We destroyed an entire nation. Instead of engaging troops, man on man, gun on gun, we attempted to kill all the women and children in the major cities so that the country would surrender. At one point MacNamara had tears in his eyes. I couldn't believe it. Robert MacNamara, with tears in his eyes.

I stood there at the window and looked out at the city, Bono going off in my speakers. War is awful. I don't know whether it was right or wrong, what we did in Japan, but I know it was awful. I realize it ended the war, and I know it saved lives in the long run, and I know about Hitler, and I know Japan wanted half the world, but that doesn't mean we shouldn't mourn war anyway, that doesn't mean we shouldn't feel a grief at the terrible ways conflicts are negotiated in a world absent God.

That morning, looking out my window, I imagined an explosion in Portland; I imagined what it would have been like to be in a war, an atomic bomb destroying the downtown skyline. I could see it in my mind: all the buildings bending in slow motion, then bursting into flames. I could see, in my mind, the after-blast of the explosion coming up from behind our house, blowing the trees so they lay against the ground where they dry instantly in the heat then flame up in coal-sticks and embers. I imagined cars lifting off the roads, light as paper, smashing into the porches of the expensive homes across Burnside. I imagined a city bus smashing through the trees that stand against Laurelhurst Park and the pond beginning to boil and the fish coming to the surface.

How do you stop a war, I wonder? I am not certain it was right for Bonhoeffer to try to kill Hitler. I am not certain it was right, but I know I would have done it myself; that if I'd had him in the crosshairs of a gun I would have pulled the trigger. I get very angry at injustice. Give me a gun and I would have killed Stalin, who slaughtered sixty million, or for that matter, Lenin. I can't think of any other solution. You can't let evil run wild, can you? War is difficult like that. It is complicated. There seems to be no right and no wrong.

Tony spent several years in Albania and literally prayed and asked God whether He wanted him to kill Slobodan Milosevic. Tony didn't do it, but he told me in a very quiet conversation at Horse Brass that he wanted to, that he sat in his room at night and imagined lying flat on a rooftop with a rifle, or getting close enough to the dictator, perhaps at an open event, to run a knife through his neck. It's ugly stuff, I know, but if Tony had done it, he would have saved millions of lives. Clinton took forever to do anything about that situation. You think you can trust a Democrat to do something about this sort of thing, but you can't.

War is no recent phenomenon, either. At times it feels like all this just started happening a few years ago, but it didn't. There were still soldiers in Vietnam when I was born, and my grandfathers' generation fought in World War II, and not long before that, World War I. Historians are divided as to whether the Trojan Wars actually happened in 1200 BC, but I believe they did. It's not that I know anything about it, I know only the heart of man, and the heart of man is going to go to war. Put a red dot in the place of a war on the timeline of world history, and there won't be a year of peace anywhere; it will all be red. After the Trojan Wars were the Persian Wars; after the Persian Wars were the Peloponnesian Wars, and then the Wars of Alexander the Great, and they go on and on. Caesar, Stalin, Lenin, Hitler, Hussein . . . they all believed they were right, defending truth, doing what was best, propagating sentiments of patriotism to a nation-state, as though God Himself believed one country any better than another.

I bring this up only because the fall of man, when Adam and Eve ate from that tree, occurred because there was a war going on. This is the only way I can explain life as we know it. The people of Japan were not monsters, they were just people, but they were caught up in war. They were victims of war, victims of a handful of men, a handful of leaders who wanted something they couldn't have.

Scripture indicates that there were wars in heaven and that Satan hates God. I realize we want to blame all the world's problems on individual responsibility, that we want to look at Scripture through a Western-financial lens, saying that everybody is responsible for everything they do, but this is only half true. Adam and Eve were deceived; they were misled. Something in them wanted something they couldn't have, but they were tricked into thinking those thoughts. It's a both/and situation. We are wired so that other people help create us, help make us who we are, and when deception is fed to us, we make bad decisions. War is complicated; it isn't black and white. That is what the Bible teaches. And I thought about that for a long time and realized it meant all our civilizations, our personalities, our families, our souls, are walking through the wreckage of a war, running from Tokyo, running from Hiroshima, our mouths gaping, the fire burning behind us, our wounds wet with blood and muddied with ash. This is Sarajevo all over again, only this time it's the walls of our hearts that are littered with bullet holes, it's our souls that are feeling the aftershock.

In a way, the war in heaven, the war between God and those against God, is the war to explain all wars. If you really want to believe one side is good and another side is bad, if you really want to look back through history and find a perfect and innocent kingdom that was attacked by an enemy, you have to go back to the Garden of Eden. A perfect and innocent kingdom hasn't been attacked since then. Details are few because Moses hardly gets into it, but to be sure, the Bible paints a picture of a certain evil tricking innocent humans into betraying the God who loved them, the King who was their friend. They were enticed, they considered their options, and they wanted to be equal to God. It's ugly stuff.

Chapter 3 of Genesis is, to me, one of the most confusing in all Scripture. I can't read it without producing a list of questions for God, questions I fear have few answers. God does not choose to tell us why He let Satan walk around in the Garden so he could talk to Adam and Eve, and He doesn't tell us why God did not talk to

Adam and Eve to kindly counsel them about Satan's deception. God might have done this, but if He did, we don't have any record of it. And while God told the sad couple in no uncertain terms to not eat from the Tree of the Knowledge of Good and Evil, He did not seem to tell them that there was such a thing as a lie, and such a being as a liar. Was this covered in the pre-earth manual? There are times when I find myself angry at the couple because all the tragedy in all of life can be traced back to them, but I also see them as somewhat innocent, having been created by God with minds that could so easily be deceived.

And yet the crime the couple committed seems unforgivable. They fell for a trick. Far from a technicality in behavior, their eating of the fruit was a heart-level betrayal between committed friends: God and man. At issue in the tragedy of the Garden is a relational crime. Adam and Eve were not satisfied with their relationship with God, and they wanted to change the dynamic by increasing their own power, a reality that simply wasn't possible, save in the fantasy realm whispered to them through the words of the evil one.

A God Betrayed

I've a friend who overheard his wife on the phone with another man. She did not know he was in the house, and he walked up behind her and leaned against the frame of the door to hear her confess her love and enjoyment of the other man's touch. My friend drove around Baltimore in a daze; he went into coffee shops and sat with his head in his hands. He went to a bus station and bought a ticket to Pittsburgh, but he missed his bus, sick from smoking a pack of cigarettes. Instead, he spent an hour in the bathroom vomiting yellow muck into a filthy toilet.

Our systematic theology reduces the fall of man to a technical act of betrayal. We hardly think of it as relational at all. But I think this view distorts what actually happened. I think God must have felt like my friend in Baltimore. I think it was something terribly painful for God to endure. I don't think we can understand the pain a pure love would feel after being betrayed by the focus of its love. You wouldn't think God would forgive them at all. You would think God would just kill them. If a couple of terrorists pulled something like that today, they might be dragged through the streets, their bodies used as human torches and hung in a public place for months. People would travel from miles away to spit on their bones.

GENESIS

When I think about God arriving in the Garden after the Fall, I think about Jimmy Carter arriving at the base of Mount Saint Helens after the eruption. It's just fifty miles across the river, Mount Saint Helens, and on a clear day you can see it from Portland. And I remember seeing Jimmy Carter getting out of his helicopter, the belly of the helicopter caked in mud, the sides of it gray with ash. Carter stepped down from his seat, his expression confused, troubled, all the pain of a region mapped in the lines of his face. And later, when I was twenty-one, I went to the place myself and tried to imagine it then. I imagined Harry Truman at Mirror Lake, refusing to leave despite the warnings. I imagined two thousand feet of this once great mountain coming down on him, sliding him and his lake over the next mountain and down the other side, displacing the body of water altogether. There were tremors, only a month of them, hardly a warning for a mountain that had sat dormant for a hundred years.

A few years ago I drove up the winding road in my car, the fresh mountain air wafting in through the windows and swirling around in the backseat, the tall pines lining the road like statues, the round, tight corners walled on one side by cliffs and the other side by thousands of feet of descent, down to a blue river bright like a mirror through the canyon, shining silver and white over rocks, then back to blue in the pools, casting up against the same-colored sky. *It was all so beautiful,* I remember thinking. And then I hit the spot on the road where the trees stopped, and the landscape went dead, like the landscape after Hiroshima, as though the place had been bombed. There was no life, not a plant, not a tree, just gray ash flowing across the hills for thirty miles toward the crater.

I rounded the long steeps toward the visitors' center, which sits on a neighboring hill, the few green trees around which were the only life on what seemed to me an ugly, dry planet. And this is precisely how I began to feel, that I was no longer on earth, that I was in some other orb with some other climate and some other ecosystem, all of which was the product of some tragedy, as though the people who inhabited this place were destroyed or, if they lived somewhere out there in the ash, were walking around in a daze, having suffered a kind of concussion, trying to make a life in the ruined landscape. The placards at the door said ash had been carried as far north as Canada. Spokane, some three hundred miles away, was deluged with more than three feet of ash. Rivers were dammed, others created, and some of the rivers, filled with walls of ash and water from Mirror Lake, took out bridges with their muscle. The Columbia, the lifeline to this region and the second largest river in the United States, was shut down completely as ash brought the bed to only twelve feet.

My friend Danielle said she encountered the sight in the parking lot after church. She was a little girl then, walking out of the sanctuary holding her father's hand and staring confusedly as a mountain she and her family had known all their lives, some fifteen miles away, spit a plume larger than the cloud over Nagasaki, going up into heaven like some angry burst of earth. They must have thought the world was coming to an end.

—

All this makes me wonder what God must have felt, arriving on the scene just after the Fall, knowing all He had made was ruined, and understanding at once the sacrifice that would be required to win the hearts of His children from the grasp of their seducer. I see Him in my mind walking the paths, calling to the couple, meeting their eyes for the first time, and Adam and Eve shaking in absolute terror, wondering what had happened, confused at the broken promise of a snake, feeling at once the trustworthiness of their first love and wondering if God would ever love them again, feeling the hot breath of His anger and emotion, hearing Him speak for the first time, not as a friend, but as One who had been betrayed. "Who told you that you were naked?"

—

Scripture would indicate that God had to break the relationship when man sinned against Him, that because His nature is purely good, purely right and lovely, He could not directly interact with beings who were, in their hearts, set against Him. This should not be confused with a lack of love, a lack of compassion; it must be understood only as two opposite natures unable to interact without one tainting the other. This is a very beautiful thing because you and I need for God to be perfectly good, we need for Him to be the voice that did one day, and will in the future, speak pure glory into our lives. But for now, because of this act of war, relations have been strained. And we are feeling it in our souls.

—

I have on my desktop a picture of a boy named Sasha. Sasha is one of the children of Chernobyl, a young boy born after the disaster that happened when the core at a nuclear facility in Russia melted and leaked. This little boy, Sasha, is perhaps five years old, and he is gripping with a tiny arm the side of a crib. His other hand is flailing upward toward his ear, his head and shoulders the only portion of his body not mutated. On the right side of Sasha's chest rises a lump the size of a softball and his belly grows out disfigured before him as though he were pregnant, a truly painful sight. His legs are oversized and blocky and he has no knees, only rounded flesh flowing awkwardly to his oversized feet, which produce four toes each, the largest of which, as big as my fist, is distanced from the others and pointing itself in an opposite direction. From the bottom of his stomach protrudes a rounded flow of flesh as though it were a separate limb, stopped in half growth. Sasha, the article in which I found the picture states, is in constant pain, lives in constant pain.

As terrible as it is to compare Sasha to ourselves, I have to go there. I have to say that you and I were not supposed to be this way. As creatures in need of somebody outside ourselves to name us, as creatures incomplete outside the companionship of God, our souls are born distorted, I am convinced of it. I am convinced that Moses was right, that his explanation was greater than Freud's or Maslow's or Pavlov's. I believe, without question, that none of us are happy in the way we were supposed to be happy. I believe that nobody on this planet is so secure, so confident in their state that they feel the way Adam and Eve felt in the Garden, before they knew they were naked. I believe we are in the wreckage of a war, a kind of Hiroshima, a kind of Mount Saint Helens, with souls distorted like the children of Chernobyl. As terrible as it is to think about these things, as ugly as it is to face them, I have to see the world this way in order for it to make sense. I have to believe something happened, and we are walking around holding our wounds.

That said, we are mistaken to believe this is a war between people with flesh and people with flesh. The only appropriate war rhetoric is war rhetoric that calls our enemies spirits, and people with flesh the victims of this war. Satan wants us to fight with one another, and I understand that sometimes evil must be restrained, but our war, the war of the ones who believe in Jesus, is a war unseen. If we could muster a portion of the patriotism we feel toward our earthly nations into a patriotism and bravery in concert with the kingdom of God, the enemy would claim fewer casualties to be sure.

Not long ago I was wrestling rather desperately with some specific passages in Scripture. To be honest, I misunderstood them and my pastor, Rick, helped me walk through them so I could understand. The specifics seem trivial now, but at the time I was experiencing a great deal of pain trying to figure out the ideas God was expressing. I have always been somewhat obsessive-compulsive in terms of not being able to turn off my mind. I get stuck on ideas and have to understand them. During this difficult time, my sleep was restless. And on a particular evening, after I had been asleep for a few hours, I was awakened. Now I want to tell you I have always been suspicious of people who say that God spoke to them in a dream.

Nothing like this has ever happened to me, and even as I type this I cannot say that what happened was actually God. I only know I had a dream that was not quite a dream. I woke up, and yet I didn't.

I was aware that I was lying in my bed, in my home, that the fan was on in the room, and yet I was also aware that I was in another place, standing on nothing, floating and yet stable, and there were three figures in monk robes standing to my right, facing me and bowing their heads in prayer. I had a sword in my hand and before I could figure out what was going on, a figure came at me at bullet speed from the distant darkness. I held out my sword and cut the figure in half and it fell into the darkness beneath me. I was startled, of course, and looked over at the figures and felt a certain knowledge that they were *for* me, that they were my friends, but they did not look up; they kept praying as dark figure after dark figure came out of the distance and I cut each of them in half. At one point during my dream I realized that my physical hands were actually clinched before my chest, and when I went to slice through a dark figure my hands jumped as the sword met resistance. The dream went on for a few minutes until I drifted off into normal sleep, waking up the next morning to remember this dream, one of the few dreams I have remembered in several years.

As I said, I am suspicious about whether God still talks to people in dreams. I hate writing this because I prefer dealing with more logical, sound ideas. And yet as the weeks have gone by since that dream, I have wondered if God wasn't telling me that you and I are in a spiritual war, that there is more going on than we understand, and that the Trinity is praying for us, for all of us as we deal with the evil one, who, Scripture teaches, roams about like a lion, searching for a kill (see 1 Peter 5:8).

I didn't feel any fear in my dream. I was calm because I knew God was there. I am not trying to get anybody worked up into any kind of worry. I tell you this story only to reiterate that I believe we are in the wreckage of a terrible act of war, and that this war is still being waged today, against what Scripture calls the principalities of darkness (see Ephesians 6:12), that is, spirits who hate God.

—

I happened to see Larry King interview Billy Graham shortly after the shootings at Columbine High School in Littleton, Colorado. I had read an article the previous month about violent video games and their effects on the minds of children, desensitizing them to the act of killing. Larry King asked Billy Graham what was wrong with the world, and how such a thing as Columbine could happen. I knew, because Billy Graham was an educated man, he had read the same article I had read, and I began calculating his answer for him, that violence begets violence, that we live in a culture desensitized to the beauty of human life and the sanctity of creation. But Billy Graham did not blame video games. Billy Graham looked Larry King in the eye and said, *"Thousands of years ago, a young couple in love lived in a garden called Eden, and God placed a tree in the Garden and told them not to eat from the tree . . ."*

And I knew in my soul he was right.

Adam, Eve, and the Alien

How the Fall Makes You Feel

I was thinking about all this the other day while my roommate Grant and I were watching a Blazers game. I was telling Grant that if I were an alien and I came down to earth from some far-off planet, there are a few things I would notice about people, and the first thing I would notice is the way they looked, that is, if people looked different on my planet. Then I would notice how their cities were constructed and, depending on how the civilization had advanced wherever I was from, I would notice how ahead or behind their cities happened to be. You know what I mean, mass transit and all, technology; but after I got over all of this and sat down to have a beer with some people, really finding out what they were interested in, what they loved and hated, there would be one thing I would notice that would kind of explain everything. And by *everything*, I mean all the stuff that makes a person want to live his life a certain way or the stuff that drives a person's thoughts, subconscious and conscious.

And I was telling Grant, "Let's say I was an alien and I had to go back to my home planet and explain to some head-of-the-aliens guy about what people on this planet were like." I told Grant that I would say to the head alien, "The thing that defines human personalities is that they are constantly comparing themselves to one another." Grant kind of nodded at me as if he thought this was interesting, then he took a sip of his beer and we went back to watching the game. But I kept thinking about this and that night I got out of bed and wrote my thoughts down on a piece of paper, you know, as if I were an alien. I put it down in a fancy alien voice:

> Humans, as a species, are constantly, and in every way, comparing themselves to one another, which, given the brief nature of their existence, seems an oddity and, for that matter, a waste. Nevertheless, this is the driving influence behind every human's social development, their emotional health and sense of joy, and, sadly, their greatest tragedies. It is as though something that helped them function and live well has gone missing, and they are pining for that missing thing in all sorts of odd methods, none of which are working. The greater tragedy is that very few people understand they have the disease. This seems strange as well because it is obvious. To be sure, it is killing them, and yet sustaining their social and economic systems. They are an entirely beautiful people with a terrible problem.

That is how an alien would see the world, in my opinion. It is obvious to me there is something wrong with us; there is something incomplete. The guy who says there isn't anything incomplete is probably the same guy who cries himself to sleep at night, or tries to get a lot of people to love him, or has terrible prejudices. We all have these tendencies, and they had to come from somewhere.

A few days later, Grant and I were watching television again and I wondered out loud what an alien would think if he came over to watch some television with us. I wondered what an alien would think of our television shows. He probably wouldn't understand any of it, because all the plots have to do with getting and finding the thing that is missing in our souls, only not getting it from God, but from other people.

If the alien wasn't missing the same thing we were missing, he would sit there in my room with Grant and me, watching basketball but not understanding why we play the game. *Why do they do that?* the alien might say. *It's a game, a competition,* Grant and I would answer. *But why? Why do they play the game? What are they trying to decide?*

They are trying to decide who is the better basketball team, Grant and I would say. *The better basketball team?* the alien might question, wondering out loud why twenty thousand people would show up to find out which basketball team was better than the other.

Feeling a little judged, Grant and I might change the channel to find that new show on E! called *Rank*, the show that ranks people from best to worst, based on some random criteria. The episode might count down to who is the most eligible bachelor, who is the hottest couple, who has the best boobs, best eyes, best smile, whatever. Then, knowing the show was again proving the alien's point, just like basketball, we might turn the channel to that show *Survivor*, and then over to *The Bachelor*, and then over to *Last Comic Standing*, or *Fear Factor*, or whatever. And then we would sort of feel bad because all of our television shows are trying to figure out who is better than who, or if they aren't, they are presupposing that one kind of person is better than another and building their comedy or their drama from this presupposition.

You guys, the alien might say, *you are obsessed. You have to wear a certain kind of clothes, drive a certain car, speak a certain way, live in a certain neighborhood, whatever, all of it so you can be higher on an invisible hierarchy. It's an obsession! You are trying to feel right by comparing yourself to others. It is ridiculous. Who told you there was anything wrong with you in the first place? Don't you know that a human is just a human?*

I kept thinking about all this, you know, what the alien was saying to Grant and me, and it caused me to wonder if this thing that makes us compare ourselves is what happened at the Fall. It occurred to me that what the alien was saying made sense because now that God was gone, now that He wasn't around to help us feel that we were loved and important and good, we were looking for it in each other, in a jury of peers.

And then I began to wonder if Adam and Eve were to visit Grant and me to watch *Survivor,* for example, how confused they might be, how they might sit around naked and look over at the alien and roll their eyes all the time, making Grant and me feel very uncomfortable. And we might say, *Well, look at your stupid system. You sit around naked all the time,* and they might look over at us as if we were the crazy ones, needing to have all kinds of fabric in our closets to put on and make ourselves look fancy and less naked, and we would say to them, *Man, you just don't get it.* And they would say to us, *Man, you just don't get it.*

And I could feel in my soul all this was true, that these were the wounds of Chernobyl, of the Fall, and I began to realize how ugly and desperate the situation actually was.

At Palio I would lean over and listen to conversations people were having with each other. People would talk about their jobs or how much money they made and they would talk about who liked them and who didn't, and how the ones who liked them were sweet and the ones who didn't were spiteful and moody and didn't have any authority about social matters. They would talk about what was cool and what wasn't, who had a better or more credible sense of taste, what they were going to do to make their house nicer, which sports team was better than which other.

And then I started thinking about my own life, how I need people to love me and like me and how, if they don't, I feel miserable and sad and how I am tempted to believe what they are saying about me is true. It is as though the voice God used to have has been taken up by less credible voices. And when I think about this I know that Genesis 3 is true; I know without a doubt I am a person who is wired so that something outside myself tells me who I am. I am not trying to say I have some kind of terrible dysfunction or anything, it's just that other people's opinions, after the Fall, have become very important, and if everybody says that Saab cars are cool, then I want a Saab car, and if people say that a certain kind of music is cool, then I am more likely to listen to that kind of music. And all this made me realize that the alien was right, and that Adam and Eve had it a great deal better before they ate the fruit.

—

I remember when I first learned about people who were and weren't cool. There was a kid in my middle school who never took a bath. He had dreadful buckteeth, so large they came out his mouth an inch, and so under no circumstances could he close his lips. I used to look at him in class and wonder how his mouth did not dry out. He kept long hair, his family too poor to afford a haircut, and he would wear the same clothes for a week, each day becoming more gray, each week his hair coming more over his eyes, and he had the jumpy feel of a beat dog. He would set his languid body over the papers on his desk, his oily hair coming over his head like a curtain, and in this position he would sit all day, talking to no one, only hoping to avoid the jury of his peers, a constant source of condemnation.

I would watch Pete during class, study him from seats behind, and reflect on his ugliness, feeling some bit of pity, but also a degree of self-righteousness. I was not a popular kid at school to be sure. I was unsightly enough to gain ridicule yet quiet enough to avoid it. Elementary school had me loud because you could get commodity from personality at that age, but middle school had the economy shifting entirely to looks, wealth, and athletic prowess. Of the three, I lacked all in equal.

Pete was something of a relief to me because I knew my proverbial backside was covered by his presence, the volume of prejudice always going toward the most different, the most repulsive, and in our school, and for this purpose, Pete took the hate. If it is the nature of man to measure himself against others, as the alien said, Pete was ever beneath us, so far beneath us, in fact, that in his presence, geeks felt like kings. The temptation for each of us to measure ourselves against Pete was insatiable in that we knew we couldn't lose in the exchange.

A child learns early there is a fashionable and an unfashionable in the world, an ugly and a pretty, a valued and an unvalued. Where this system comes from, God only knows, but it is rarely questioned, and though completely illogical and agreed upon by everyone as evil, it remains in play, commanding our emotions as a possession. It isn't something taught to us by our parents; it is something that comes naturally, as though a radioactive kind of tragedy happened, screwing up our souls. Adulterated or policed, the system can grow to something more civilized, but no less dominant as a drive of nature. In youth the system is obvious. If you want to learn the operating system to which humans are subjected, step into a classroom of preteen students and listen to the dialogue. You will hear the constant measurements, the talk about family wealth, whose father drives what car, who lives in what neighborhood, or who is dating whom.

Here is how it feels: From the first day of school the conversation is the same as it would be if hundreds of students were told to stand in line ranging from best to worst, coolest to most uncool, each presenting their case for value, each presenting an offense to the cases of others, alliances being formed as caricatures of reality television (or vice versa).

And here is what is terrible: There will be a sort of punishment being dealt to those at the end of the line, each person dealing out castigation as a way of dissociation from the geeks, driven by the fear that associating with somebody at the end of the line might cost them position, as if the two might be averaged, landing each of them in the space between. And so, in this way, students are constantly looking to associate themselves with those higher in line, and dissociate from those of low position. Great lengths will be taken to associate with those at the front of the line. Students will kiss up, drop names, lie about friendships, and so on. Many will hate the most popular, and yet subject themselves to their approval as though they were small gods. But the great crime, the great tragedy, is not in the attempts to associate but rather in the efforts to dissociate. If a person feels his space in the hierarchy is threatened, that he might lose position, the vehemence he feels toward the lesser person is nearly malevolent.

I say all this only because the torture Pete knew from us was unrelenting. I remember a scene with him backed against his locker surrounded by jocks, my friends and I feeling somehow powerful, not because we were joining the harassment, but because we were not the victims of it. We were horrible to him, if you want to know the truth, but it felt as though we had to be, that by ridiculing Pete we were protecting ourselves from some terrible fate.

The feeling was that if we were last on the social ladder, or near last, we would be facing some kind of torture. Though it sounds absurd, it *felt* true, as though there were a spirit in the air directing our passions. It was incredibly important to climb this ladder, and the closer you were to the top, it was believed, the easier you could breathe, because at the top people loved you and cared about you and gave you a little bit of the thing God used to give you.

—

Pete was last on the list of valuable people at my school. The ones who were first were the blonde girls, the girls who would become cheerleaders, and after the cheerleaders were the tall, athletic boys who would become football players. Soccer girls came after football boys, but not by much. They were an interesting set, very beautiful with tanned legs of muscle, and if they'd wanted they could have been as valuable as cute blondes, but they chose not to; they chose to play soccer and dress granola as if they didn't care. But they dated the same boys the blondes dated, and each time an athlete and a granola would connect, the school considered them a beautiful novelty because, to some degree, each of them was showing grace to the other.

Small graces like these were meaningful in middle school. They stated that the walls separating social classes, though they were tall, could be mounted by that mysterious thrust of hormones we ignorantly referred to as love.

Pam dated Nick, for instance, and William hooked up with Ivy, Kelly made out with Sam on the trip to the Museum of Natural

History and came back with a crush on Jim, Sam's best friend, who, the entire time Kelly and Sam were making out on the bus, sat two seats in front of them in tears. Romantic relationships in middle school, though driven to some degree by pure emotions, were much more negotiations within the ladder, each party asking for trust from the other, the entire school acting as an audience for the grand play of life. And we ate and drank this drama. There was much to be gained and lost in these exchanges. For instance, the relationship between Kelly and Jim lasted an astounding eight months, all the way through the winter production of *A Christmas Carol*, during the practices for which Jim, who played the Ghost of Christmas Past, fell for Rachel, who played Mrs. Cratchet. Rumors of the relationship were denied by Jim straight to Kelly's face, but confirmed with a bold kiss at curtain call on opening night, sending Kelly, in complete hysterics, to the girls' restroom off the gym side of the auditorium, the bellows from which proved more dramatic, in fact, than the fellow in the play who got his bearings about the meaning of Christmas. It was great stuff, I have to tell you, but I didn't even think way back then about how this drama was being created because certain forces or desires existed within us and those desires had an explanation.

We were lost in the drama. We never wondered about where it all came from or why it existed. And we talked about these matters as heads of state might discuss international policy. We sat in the lunchroom and talked about who was going out with whom and who was going to get beat up after school, and who had a big house in a nice neighborhood. Lunch was our AP wire, and we mulled over the daily fare in contemplation and awe, always wondering where the shifts had taken place on the invisible ladder.

When it was hinted that barriers had been breached, that invisible lines had been crossed in the categories of important and unimportant, mayhem ensued. Kim Morgan, for instance, on a dare, kissed Mark Bryant on the cheek. Kim played on the soccer team and Mark kept quiet and to himself and wasn't anything like a jock, only known for the company he kept with a group of computer geeks who played Dungeons and Dragons on the kickball field during lunch.

Here is how it happened: A clique of girls gathered across from Mark's locker, his short stature just enough for his eyes to find the bottom of his stacked books, a foundation for rotten lunches, crumpled papers, and gym clothes. Kim approached him from behind, said his name, and as he turned she went in for the deed. Mark jerked back, closed his eyes, and held his breath in one reaction. Kim shriveled in disgust when she was done. She wiped her lips on the arm of her sweater and released a breathy scream the tone of bus brakes.

News of the event rippled through the school like scandal, and for two days a few of the gaggle close to Kim splintered and would not talk to her. But my friends and I loved her for what she had done. Though it was only a dare and could not be confused with a sincere act of affection, she had broken the invisible social barrier.

That evening I wondered if Kim's kiss would make an impact on social partitions. A valuable person had crossed the line to kiss a person of no value. Maybe they would realize we were all just humans, I thought; maybe they would realize the feelings about the hierarchy were not true, that we were somehow equal, a computer nerd and a football player, the same.

But the system remained. It seemed while no logical evidence existed for one group of people being of more importance than another, feelings, not thought, governed the hierarchy. And time would show us all how severe, how passionate these feelings could grow.

—

Pete, the fellow I told you about earlier who did not bathe or cut his hair, had learned walking patterns that allowed him to, for the most part, blend in. If a group of athletes were coming toward him, he would walk briskly, close to the lockers, always looking down and away. And most of the time the athletes honored his request and left him alone.

One day after school, however, Pete's mother was late to pick him up. Pete's family had a station wagon caked with mud and filled, in the back, with stacks of newspapers. Pete stood under the overhang at the door, away from the bicycle rack where everybody else waited for his or her parents. I knew that Pete could feel he was in danger, because he did not look directly at the bike rack. He would, only on occasion, glance over as a defense.

Phil the Pope's parents were also late that day. Phil was not king of the jocks, but he was friends with the king, and he always had flyers for the dances at the Catholic church, flyers for bazaars and special events, and as he walked down the hall he would slap them against my chest, look me in the eye, and say, "You don't have anything going on Saturday night, Miller; come to the bazaar at the Catholic church. I'll be looking for you." Phil did this sort of thing under the direction of his mother, who was the church's secretary.

Phil the Pope was loud, strong, violent, and named you if you looked at him. Meet his eye and he would say *geek*, *fatso*, *dork*, or some other expletive demeaning who you were as a person. Praise from Phil was silence. If he did not know what you were, he would look away when he walked by. If he was still deciding, he would nod his head in an impulsive up motion (decisions leaning toward geek were combined with parted lips; decisions leaning toward fashionable were mingled with a faint, though not disarming, half-smile).

On that day at the bike rack, Phil was gathering those in the social class beneath him, those who were athletic but did not like sports, girls who would not become cheerleaders but would be accepted to the drill team, and he was holding Jeff Markum's backpack away from him, Jeff laughing with Phil, wrestling and trying to get his books. That is when the terrible thing happened. In a defensive glance from Pete, he and Phil met eyes. I saw it happen from across the street where my friends and I were standing. Phil set the bag on the ground and said some things to the people standing around him. And then Phil bolted from the group toward Pete, followed by several other boys.

Pete tried to get back inside the building where he would be protected by teachers but Phil caught him, pulled him off the door, the handle of which was held so tightly by Pete it nearly broke off. Boys stood before the windows on the door as Phil buried his fists in Pete's stomach and chest, kicking him to the ground and unleashing such a great force of aggression and hate that the sight of it stopped my breath. And I'll tell you this, the violence in film does not depict the sudden bursts with which most pain is dealt; the quick hits to the face, the crack of knuckles on skull, the blood pumped from lips and buckteeth, the profanities and insults coming up from some deep, gut place of horrors. My friends and I ran across the street. We jumped at Phil, several of us, and yelled for him to step off. Pete's face was covered in blood and he was screaming, terrified, screaming and swinging his fists blindly as a lens of blood bubbled over his eyes.

Phil rose to his feet, bent over to catch his breath, looked down at Pete, and spit in his face. And then he disappeared around the corner of the building.

Pete's mother came only a few minutes later, and we all helped Pete into the nurse's office where he was swabbed with a wet towel. I distinctly remember Pete's mother ridiculing Pete, telling him he was always finding trouble, always causing a scene. Pete cried out that it wasn't his fault, and we agreed, quite passionately saying that it had been Phil the Pope, but Pete's mother would have none of it. She kept looking at her son in disgust. The nurse, confused, said it would be best if we went to the office where the principal was questioning students. And as we walked out of the room I remember feeling that Pete bore more fear of his mother than of any of us, even Phil the Pope.

Some people get the worst of it, it's true. You grow up being told that all people are created equal, but they aren't. Some people are born into better homes than others, and some people look better than others, and some people are smarter and some people run faster.

In the end, Phil the Pope was suspended for a week for fighting. Pete didn't come back to school for two days, and when he returned he had bruises from the fight with Phil as well as another collection I wondered if he had received at home. We all felt so sorry for him. After the thing with Phil the Pope happened, I used to look at Pete in class and wonder about how unfair life was, about how things weren't right. Nobody made fun of him again, to his face or behind his back. While the social barriers were still in play, defended with ignorant passion, Pete was exempt. His family moved away two years later, and I suspect he played the same role at whatever school he went to next, only without the grace we felt obliged to show him. But for us, and for those two years, he was treated with as much respect as our system could allow a person of his stature. We quietly ignored him.

If I could do it again, knowing what I know now, I would be

his friend. I would have defended him. But I was no brilliant kid and I had no idea that the emotions we were feeling were not true, that what we were doing was wrong.

I get this feeling sometimes that after the world ends, when God destroys all our buildings and our flags, we will wish we had seen everybody as equal, that we had eaten dinner with prostitutes, held them in our arms, opened up spare rooms for them and loved them and learned from them. I was just another stupid child in the flow, you know; I didn't know any of these things. I didn't know it didn't matter what a person looked like, how much money they made or whether or not they were cool. I didn't know that cool was just a myth and that one person was just as beautiful and meaningful as another. Not all of us are as smart as aliens, you know. Not all of us run around naked like Adam and Eve. You can hardly fault me for this stuff, can you? Like I said, it felt important to climb the social ladder, it felt important to defend our identities, it felt as though we were saving our own lives.

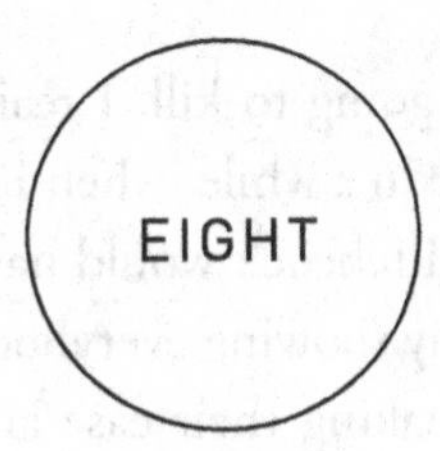

Lifeboat Theory

How to Kill Your Neighbor

When I was a kid in elementary school my teacher, Mrs. Wunch, asked our class a question that I've come back to about a million times, trying to figure out an answer. The question she asked went along with a lesson about *Values Clarification*, which is a fancy name for learning how to be a snob. This is how the question went:

"If there were a lifeboat adrift at sea, and in the lifeboat were a male lawyer, a female doctor, a crippled child, a stay-at-home mom, and a garbageman, and one person had to be thrown overboard to save the others, which person would we choose?"

I don't remember which person we threw out of the boat. I think it came down to the lawyer, but I can't remember exactly. I do remember, however, that the class did not hesitate in deciding who had value and who didn't. The idea that all people are equal never came up. As I was saying before, we knew this sort of thing intrinsically. Or at least we thought we did.

I ordered an Alfred Hitchcock film the other day off Amazon called *Lifeboat* because I was thinking about Mrs. Wunch and how she wanted us to figure out whom we were going to kill. I really like a good black-and-white movie every once in a while, when I'm in a certain mood, and I figured old Alfred Hitchcock would have a pretty good take on the plot, you know, really showing everybody trying not to get thrown out of the boat, making their case and that sort of thing. It turns out the film wasn't about that at all because the lifeboat in the film was plenty big, and the people were rescued before anybody died. There was one girl who killed herself because her baby had drowned, and another guy got murdered, but mostly it was just a lot of melodramatic dialogue in the way of old black-and-white movies.

The movie was pretty boring, to be honest, and it didn't give me what I wanted. I wanted to feel what it would be like to explain to everybody else in a lifeboat why you shouldn't be thrown overboard. The reason I wanted to feel this was because I wondered if those emotions, the emotions you would feel in a lifeboat, were anything like the feelings we all feel when we are living our lives, just hanging out at the house or going to the grocery store.

The thing is, if people are in a lifeboat, the reason they feel passionately about being a good person and all is because if they aren't, they are going to be thrown overboard; they are going to be killed. I realize that sounds grim, but I kept comparing, in my mind, the conversation that might take place in a lifeboat with the conversations I heard at Palio or at Horse Brass. Because when you really think about it, these wants we have, like wanting to be right, wanting to be good, wanting to be perceived as humble, wanting to be important to people, and wanting to be loved, feel perilous, as though by not getting them something terrible is going to happen.

People wouldn't get upset about being disrespected if there weren't some kind of penalty in play.

For instance, there was a guy at Palio the other day who was standing in line and somebody cut in front of him and so he got very upset, rolled his eyes and all, and stood there with his hands in his pockets nearly staring a hole through the back of the guy's head who had stepped in front of him. And the thing I was thinking was, *Who cares, you know? It's only going to cost you about two minutes for that guy's coffee to get made, then you can get yours,* but then I thought about the whole lifeboat thing, and how if somebody says you aren't important, and if somebody cuts in front of you in line, it feels like a terrible thing is happening to you, and you would be mad at that guy because you would feel that he was costing you something, that there is a kind of penalty for not being important.

I have a friend who gets so terribly upset when somebody pulls in front of him when he is driving that he will nearly turn red, and beat his steering wheel, yelling at the guy who pulled in front of him. That is pretty crazy because somebody cutting in front of you on the road is only going to cost you a second but it feels like something more; it feels like there is a penalty for not being respected by other people, it feels like you are going to die unless you get some kind of respect and appreciation.

In this way, the alien was right; we are comparing ourselves to one another and if somebody says they are better than you, it makes you very frustrated inside and you get sad or angry or bitter about it.

And that made so much sense in light of what Moses was saying in Genesis 3, it bears repeating: God wired us so that He *told* us who we were, and outside that relationship, the relationship that said we were loved and valuable and beautiful, we didn't have any worth at all. As horrible as it sounds, it would make sense that things of worth are things God loves, and things that don't have worth are things God doesn't love. I mean, I really started wondering if maybe a human is defined by who loves him. I know it sounds terrible, because we have always grown up believing that a person is valuable even if nobody loves them, and I certainly agree with that because God made everybody and the Bible very clearly states He loves everybody. But, as Paul said, if those relations are disturbed, the relations between God and man, then we feel the desire to be loved and respected by other people instead of God, and if we don't get that love and respect, we feel very sad or angry because we know that our glory is at stake, that if there isn't some glory being shone through us by somebody who has authority, we'll be dead inside, like a little light will go out and our souls will feel dark, like nothing can grow there. We'll feel that there is a penalty, by default, for being removed from love.

I know this makes God sound like a terrible narcissist, but my friend John MacMurray said to me recently that the most selfless thing God could do, that is, the most selfless thing a perfect Being who is perfectly loving could do, would be to create other beings to enjoy Himself.

Even Jesus says His glory comes from the Father, which I take to mean that even Christ, a perfect Being, was valuable because God loved Him. And I realize that this sounds weak and codependent, but what if a person isn't supposed to be alone, isn't supposed to have glory on his own, but rather get glory from the God who loves him? What if, in the same way the sun feeds plants, God's glory gives us life? What if our value exists because God takes pleasure in us?

Tony has this old icon on his wall, an old painting he bought in Albania that has a picture of the Trinity on it. He says the painting is a picture of the ideas presented in John 17, ideas that suggest the Trinity loves one another and is constantly telling the other guys in the Trinity they are great, they are beautiful, and in this way they are *one.* And Jesus, also in John 17, prays the disciples God gave Him would learn to live this way, and that those who are lost will be invited into this community, will want to live in this community because there is love in this community, because the way they are wired will be fulfilled, that they will be told who they are by God and God's glory will shine through them, giving them value and worth and a feeling they are loved.

I know it isn't a very Marlboro-man way to live your life, but what if the Marlboro-man way of life really sucks and makes you lonely all the time, and what if the way of Jesus, God, and the Holy Spirit, not to mention the disciples, is right; by that I mean what if the way the Trinity operates explains the way humans are wired, and that we will be fulfilled when we are finally with God and, in His companionship, we know who we are? What if when we are with God, we feel that we have glory, we feel His love for us and know, in a way infinitely more satisfying than a parent's love or a lover's love, that we matter?

I think that would be very beautiful and if I could press a button and go back to the way it was in the Garden of Eden, I would, because so many times I don't feel like I have any glory at all. I feel like I am in a lifeboat trying to get other people to say I am important and valued, and even when they do, it feels as though their opinion isn't strong enough to give me the feeling I need, the feeling that quit at the Fall.

Do you know the easiest part of the gospel of Jesus for me to believe? The part that says *the wages of sin is death* (see Romans 6:23). I take that to mean when Adam and Eve sinned, when Chernobyl happened in the Garden, from that point on Adam and Eve began to die, not only physically, but in their souls, too, because they had been separated from God. It makes sense that if a plant is separated from the sun, it dies, and that if people are separated from

God, they die. And so now it feels as if we live on a planet where there is just a little bit of water left, poisoned as it is, and we all are trying to get it and drink it so we can stay alive. But what we really need is God. What we really need is somebody who loves us so much we don't worry about death, about our hair thinning, about other drivers pulling in front of us on the road, about whether people are poor or rich, good-looking or ugly, about whether we feel lonely, or about whether or not we are wearing clothes. We need this; we need this so we can love other people purely and not for selfish gain, we need this so we can see everybody as equals, we need this so our relationships can be sincere, we need this so we can stop kicking ourselves around, we need this so we can lose all self-awareness and find ourselves for the first time, not by realizing some dream, but by being told who we are by the only Being who has the authority to know, and by that I mean the Creator.

Earlier, when I said Moses explained all of humanity, I meant without God we are, by default, in the lifeboat. And if you think about it, if we aren't in a lifeboat, that is, if these things aren't true and if this story isn't happening to us, then emotions like pride, jealousy, distrust, and embarrassment should be foreign to us. We should feel like the alien, or like Adam and Eve sitting around naked watching television, none of it making any sense.

I know this all sounds crazy. But, once again, can you think of any other reason we wear clothes? Skin is more waterproof than GORE-TEX, you know.

—

Listen to the conversations you have for the next week or so. If you are like me, you'll probably hear a hidden conversation beneath the real conversation. Stuff like movies and food and people become ideas, and we all are deciding whether we're on the right or wrong side of these ideas, knowing that if we aren't on the right side, there is a price to pay. For instance, if you walk into the living room where your wife is or your roommate is and you say something like, *Hey, Margaret, you know the other day when you said you liked enchiladas, well, I just wanted you to know that people who like enchiladas are dorks. It's true; I read a report out of a magazine, and it says that if you like enchiladas, you were most likely a geek in school and have trouble in relationships, you know, getting people to like you.*

I'll bet you, if I did that, Margaret would get upset. Even though the idea is unfounded, it doesn't matter. The jury of peers has spoken, and so the threat has been made.

A friend pointed out recently that here in 16ortland, when the Trailblazers win a basketball game, we fans will often say *we* won, but if the team loses, we say *they* lost. The reason we do this, my friend said, is to associate ourselves with winning and dissociate ourselves from losing. In the lifeboat, associating with losers can cost you your life. When talking about sports, the phenomenon is innocent enough, but what if we're talking about politics or policy or truth or religion? I have several friends who subscribe to a certain political way of thinking, supporting only one party, and when I ask them why, they don't know, or they express a certain empty kind of rhetoric. It seems to me that many of us just chose a team years ago and are unwilling to concede that their team isn't right. So often decisions aren't being made based on whether or not the ideas of a political party are good ideas; decisions are based on associations and dissociations in the lifeboat. It becomes very dangerous.

Watch CNN for an hour and you'll see what I mean. There are about one in a million people who see life as complex, knowing that all men have the capacity to do both good and bad, to be responsible and irresponsible, but the other million think people, politicians, whatever, are perfect or entirely evil. I have Christian friends who hated Bill Clinton and love George Bush, and liberal friends who love John Kerry and can't stand George Bush. And if you listen to conservative or liberal radio, you will hear one side making fun of the other in the lifeboat. The talk will have very little to do with the issues. People see what they want to see based on what associations are going to help them survive.

No wonder the alien rolled his eyes.

And all this, of course, explains the way we treated Pete in middle school. When lifeboat conversations are about movies or music or politics, that is one thing, but what if we use people, say that people are worthless or losers in order to dissociate?

I was thinking a great deal about all this, doing some research in the library at Reed College, and I ran across an article by Emory Cowen in the *Journal of Clinical and Consulting Psychology*. The article reports that the level of popularity a child experiences in the third grade is the greatest predictor of that child's mental health when he or she reaches adulthood. A child being accepted by peers, argues Cowen, is a more sure indication of success than positive evaluation from teachers and nurses, high scores or IQ, and even psychological evaluations. And Daniel Goleman, in his book *Emotional Intelligence,* claims that the high school dropout rate of children who are rejected by their peers is between two and eight times greater than that of children who are accepted.

It would be prudent to summarize a few ideas that have brought us to this dilemma. If a human being is wired so that something outside himself gives him life, and if a separation from that something would cost him his life (physically, but also spiritually), then a human personality would seek a kind of redemption from a jury of his peers, and a lifeboat mentality would ensue across all cultures. And while Darwinian survival mechanisms may explain some of this, these explanations cannot explain the odd complexity of our interpersonal negotiations, not to mention our tendency toward clothing. Indeed, a formulaic expression of Christian theology seems slight and irrelevant when contrasted with the holistic understandings of God's message to humanity, a message of truth and meaning.

That said, an understanding of Christianity as an identity in the lifeboat by which we compare ourselves to others is entirely inappropriate. This faith is larger than the lifeboat, outside of it, you might say. Jesus would indicate the greatest thing you and I can do to display we know Him is to love our brothers and sisters unconditionally, to love our neighbors as ourselves, and to love our enemies.

It makes you feel that as a parent the most important thing you can do is love your kids, hold them and tell them you love them because, until we get to heaven, all we can do is hold our palms over the wounds. I mean, if a kid doesn't feel he is loved, he is going to go looking for it in all kinds of ways. He is going to want to feel powerful or important or tough, and she is going to want to feel beautiful and wanted and needed. Give a kid the feeling of being loved early, and they will be better at negotiating that other stuff when they get older. They won't fall for anything stupid, and they won't feel a kind of desperation all the time in their souls. It is no coincidence that Jesus talks endlessly about love. Free love. Unconditional love.

How to Survive Without God

If you ask me, the kinds of things you have to do in the lifeboat in order to not get left behind are absurd. Things were better in the Garden, to be sure. As crazy as it might have been to walk around naked, at least we didn't have to panic all the time, trying to figure out if we were loved.

Here are some of the things the alien pointed out to Grant and me, you know, about how to be loved on earth. And I must confess, when he said these things it did take me aback a bit.

- SLA13-DUNKING A BASKETBALL: Athletes will often pound their chests as if to say, *Look at me, look at me, look what I did. This is why I am important in the lifeboat.* And if you think about it, the reason they probably feel so great about doing that is not only because it is difficult to do, but more likely because thousands of cheering fans (a jury of peers) deem this valuable. Outside that, it's kind of a dud. You're just jumping in the air to put a ball through a hoop. Often, in fact, when an athlete is interviewed after a game, his one-minute speech sounds hauntingly like a case for his importance. When somebody says, "It's only a game," it reminds us of what is so easy to forget. There is some other commodity in play, some hidden commodity that the player, the fans, the coaches, and the other team all are vying for. After all, if you win the whole thing, you only get a ring. You can always buy a ring. What we really want is for the jury of our peers to give us a feeling of security.
- GOOD LOOKS: Though it may seem normal for you and me to base worth on looks, the system is actually as absurd as the alien says it is. What is beautiful, after all? And I am not

saying beauty isn't good, because it is; God made it, but using it to compare one person to another is not something, I believe, that occurred in the Garden. Beauty became a kind of point system to determine worth when the relationship with God was broken.

- INTELLIGENCE: For more than a year my friend Curt and I would meet several times a week to play chess at a local coffee shop. If I happened to win, I would leave feeling somehow secure in my identity and, very oddly, if I lost, I would feel sad or frustrated for an hour or more. While some degree of intelligence is necessary for survival, I think the alien would point out that people with mental disabilities are at times more happy than people of normal intelligence. The game of chess, for me, had become a testing or measurement of yet another commodity within the lifeboat.
- WEALTH: Humans are the only species to insatiably accumulate wealth. Sometimes I watch the MTV show *Cribs* and, if I'm not sucked in, I have to scratch my head as to why one individual would bury himself in so much stuff. Birds don't build six-story nests with heated pools. But I was thinking that in the lifeboat, currency becomes a point system by which we compare ourselves to our peers just like beauty and smarts. The phrase "keeping up with the Joneses" makes no sense outside a lifeboat context.
- RIGHTNESS: Not long ago my friend Tony and I were talking about the film *Antwone Fisher*. Tony asked if I liked the film and I told him I didn't. I listed reasons I felt the film was lacking, and Tony was taken aback. He had seen the movie the night before and was moved to tears by its ending. Our "discussion" became something close to an argument as he

> and I disagreed about the movie's quality. Somewhere in the middle of the conversation, though, we realized we had taken something as trivial as a film and brought it into the lifeboat, trying to decide who was right.

Again, the list goes on. It seems the human psyche will measure itself against anything a group of people deems a valid indicator of importance. I listed only a few, but the truth is, there are a million more.

Last year I caught an interview with Tom Arnold regarding his book *How I Lost Five Pounds in Six Years.* The interviewer asked why he had written the book, and I was somewhat amazed at the honesty of Arnold's answer. The comedian stated that most entertainers are in show business because they are broken people, looking for affirmation. "The reason I wrote this book," Tom Arnold said, "is because I wanted something out there so people would tell me they liked me. It's the reason behind almost everything I do." I have to tell you, after that, I really liked Tom Arnold. Leave it to an ex-alcoholic to tell the truth about life.

A few weeks later I was giving an interview in Seattle when the host asked me the same question asked of Tom Arnold: "Why did you write this book?" I wondered, on the air, if the explanation Tom Arnold gave was not the same reason I do what I do, and in the end, I had to concede my motives of faith often take a backseat to my broken nature and desire to feel validity in life. I told the guy in Seattle that I am broken, that I like to write, but basically, subconsciously, I just want people to like me. The guy in Seattle leaned back in his chair, paused for a moment, and said, "You aren't alone."

—

While writing books and dunking basketballs may be harmless pursuits, when the internal lifeboat mechanism goes on the defensive, when people feel threatened, feel that their lives are at stake unless they are respected, tragedy ensues.

I was speaking to a group of students at George Fox University a few months ago and asked the question *Why is racism?* Some of the students proceeded to tell me what racism was, but I had to stop them. "The question was *Why is racism?* that is, *Why does it happen?*" The room fell silent for several minutes until I offered an explanation. If there are ten people in the lifeboat, and three of them are Jews, adhering to a philosophy that Jews are inferior is enticing. If Jews or Americans or Democrats or whoever are inferior, then I am automatically ahead of 30 percent of the population in the lifeboat. Racism and socioeconomic prejudice would be the very first thing to start happening in a culture absent God. Not simply because people are "bad" but because a certain system of internal mechanisms would immediately ensue. In fact, without the model of the lifeboat, there isn't much of an explanation for the phenomenon now playing itself out in Sudan. In the context of the lifeboat (motivated by self-preservation), the characteristics of "other people" become inferior simply because they are not our characteristics. Logic is thrown out the window, or worse, used as a tool to validate our prejudices. Philosophies, ideals, and even religious convictions become weapons for slaughter.

In my own life, I notice I validate people who like or validate me. When I say so-and-so is a nice person, what I really mean is so-and-so thinks I am a nice person. And if I sense a person doesn't like me, or thinks he is better than me, my mind will find all sorts of criticism, noticing his temper or his dense intellect. After all, how many people do we dislike who don't dislike us as well? Could the reason really be their lack of character, or do these feelings come from a threatened position in the lifeboat? Don't we find humble people more companionable than arrogant people? Would we even know of these terms without a lifeboat scenario in play?

All this is to say that when the Bible indicates life comes from God, and death comes from separation from God, it makes complete sense, and this truth serves as an explanation for all of our feelings, for the way in which we interact, for the ways in which we entertain ourselves, and for the general precepts of the human plot. Without Him, we feel that we are being thrown out of a boat. No life can exist outside the influence of the sun, outside the energy of light. It makes you wonder if our souls are any different. It makes you wonder if there is any hope.

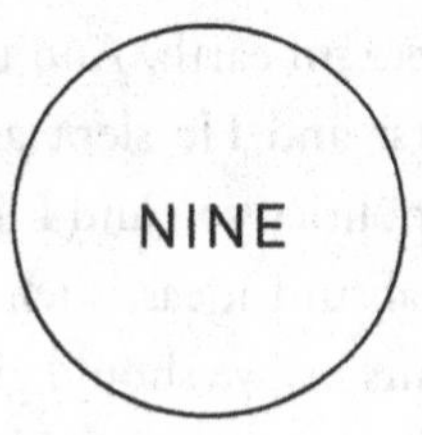

Jesus

Who Needs a Boat?

It would be very interesting if Jesus, who said He was the Son of God, understood life on earth the same way the alien did. Think about that for a second. If Jesus was coming from a place where all emotional needs were met by God, His social economy would be as shocking and different as the social economy in the Garden or on whatever planet the alien came from. His values would be different and His personality would be different.

What I mean is, if it is true that our personalities are similar to the way they would be in a lifeboat, because of the fall of man, then Jesus would act and think completely differently than we would. He would act and think like somebody who had their needs met by God, like somebody who had no regard for what we thought was important or not important. He would find the things humanity finds valuable and worthless absurd, and to the person in the lifeboat, Jesus would seem to see things backward.

I was thinking a great deal about this, so I read through the Gospels about ten times each, just to get a feel for what Jesus was like. I was asking myself while I was reading whether or not Jesus had many of the personality traits we have here on earth. And the truth is, He didn't. He had hunger and thirst and He slept and rested, but He had no regard for the lifeboat politics you and I live within every day. He believed a great many absurd ideas, such as we should turn the other cheek if somebody hits us, we should give somebody our coat even if they just ask for our shirt, we should be willing to give up all our money and follow Him, we should try our hardest to make peace, we should treat poor people the same as we treat the rich, we should lay down our lives for our friends, and so on and so on. It seemed He believed we should take every opportunity to fail in the lifeboat game, not for the sake of failing, but because there wasn't anything to win in the first place. It was as if He didn't believe the economy we live within had validity. No part of Him was deceived by its power.

—

Reading through the Gospels was one of the greatest things that ever happened to me. I know how strange it sounds to say it, but Jesus saved my faith. Several years ago I was getting to the point that the enormous, entangling religion of Christianity, with its many divisions, its multiple theologies, its fondness for war rhetoric, and its quirky, lumbering personality, was such a nuisance I hardly wanted anything to do with it.

But then I saw this very beautiful film about Martin Luther, a German monk who started the Reformation, and before he started the Reformation, when he had yet to read a copy of the Bible, he used to pace around in his room and beg God to forgive him. He would beat himself up and argue with Satan and basically act pretty screwed up, but then later, when he was able to read a copy of the Bible himself, he realized that all his redemption came through Christ, that what he really needed to do was place all his love and faith in Christ and Christ would take care of everything because Christ loved him.

This meant a great deal to me because there are, honestly, about a million ways Christians worship and about that many ways different groups say a person becomes a Christian. Trusting Christ, really placing all my faith in Him the way Martin Luther did, seemed quite meaningful and simple. It also seemed relational, not formulaic, and as I have said, my gut tells me the key to life is relational, not propositional.

—

The first thing that hit me when I started reading through the Gospels was the thought that Jesus had come to earth in the first place. Like the alien, He had it good where He was but He sacrificed it all and became a man. I suspect our mental pictures of God in heaven, of what Jesus looked like and His general composition, are not very accurate. My guess is He was quite amazing in His previous state, that He was quite happy, always surrounded by beings who loved Him, always feeling the fulfillment that an intimacy with His Father would give Him, always having God's glory shining through Him, sitting on a throne in a place of honor. The mystery of what Christ was before He was human is one of the greatest mysteries of all time, and one that will not be solved until we have new bodies, new eyes, new hearts, new minds, and strong souls with which to engage any place near Him. To exchange heaven for a *place*, and to exchange eternity for *time*, was an act of humility I don't think any of us can understand.

I was reading Brian Greene's book *The Elegant Universe*, in which the Columbia professor talks about potentials of the superstring theory. It is a very fancy book, but I was struck at one point when Greene indicated the possibility that multiple dimensions may be laid out against each other as slices of a loaf of bread or tissues in a great brain. And while distantly scientific (strings are too small to actually see and prove scientifically and have been *seen* only through mathematical formulas), the theory had me pondering about the greatness, or I should say the *otherness*, of God. I began to wonder how odd it would be if we existed in the mind of God, as Brian Greene, perhaps unknowingly, suggests. I am not saying I believe this is true, but something as radical as this, as foreign to our minds, certainly may be. And out of this other place, this other existence, Christ stepped to inhabit ours.

If you believe Jesus was God, and He came to earth to walk among us, the first thing you start considering is that He might actually care. Why else would something so great become something so small? He didn't close Himself off in a neighborhood with the Trinity; He actually left His neighborhood and moved into ours, like a very wealthy and powerful man moving to the slums of Chicago or Houston or Calcutta, living on the streets as a peasant.

I started thinking about the idea my friend at the Bible college suggested about how, if God is a perfect and loving Being, the most selfless thing He could do would be to create other beings to enjoy Him. And then I started thinking that if those creatures fell away from Him, the most selfless thing a perfect and loving Being could do would be to go and get them, to try to save them from the death that would take place in His absence.

That said, if Christ was who He said He was, and He represents an existence, a community, and an economy that are better than ours, and it is important that I "believe in Him," what is He like?

As I read the Gospels and other books about Jesus, I started a little list of personality traits and beliefs I thought were interesting. Here they are:

He Believed All People Were Equal

In reading the Gospels of the Bible, I discovered that the personality of Christ was such that people who were pagans, cultists, money-mongers, broken, and diseased felt comfortable in His presence. All this goes back to the idea of the lifeboat and how Jesus, outside that system, wouldn't believe one person was any better than another. Apparently this counterintuitive belief system was obvious in the character of Christ. In the Gospels, Jesus is always surrounded by the poor, by the marginalized. And, conversely, He is often opposed by the powerful. Not all the powerful, but those who oppose Him are almost always the people who are ahead in the lifeboat. In this way, Jesus disrupted the system by which people were gaining their false redemption.

Phillip Yancey, a writer I admire a great deal, taught a class at his church in Chicago about Jesus. He reflects on what he discovered about Jesus in his book *The Jesus I Never Knew:*

> The more unsavory the characters, the more at ease they seemed to feel around Jesus. People like these found Jesus appealing: a Samaritan social outcast, a military officer of the tyrant Herod, a quisling tax collector, a recent hostess to seven demons.
>
> In contrast, Jesus got a chilly response from more respectable types. Pious Pharisees thought him uncouth and worldly, a rich young ruler walked away shaking his head, and even the open-minded Nicodemus sought a meeting under the cover of darkness.

> I remarked to the class how strange this pattern seemed, since the Christian church now attracts respectable types who closely resemble the people most suspicious of Jesus on earth. What has happened to reverse the pattern of Jesus' day? Why don't sinners *like* being around us?

This makes a great deal of sense if you think about it, because Jesus was offering redemption through a relationship with Himself, and for those who were already being redeemed by a jury of their peers, people like politicians or wealthy people or powerful religious leaders, the redemption Jesus offered must have felt like a step down; but for those who had nothing, for those who were being threatened in the lifeboat, Jesus offered everything. In fact, at one point Christ says that it is easier for a camel to get through the eye of a needle than it is for a rich man to enter the kingdom of God. He says that a man like this will have trouble seeing the beauty of Christ on his own, and that he will need God's help. (See Luke 18:25–27.)

He Was Ugly

I remember hearing stories about Christ as a child in Sunday school, the descriptions of Him being nearly magical, having eyes that would draw people toward Him and an aura that gave people the feeling they were in the company of greatness. This led me to assume Jesus was good-looking. There was a boy at my school who made people feel this way and he was good-looking, and a girl who also was good-looking would quiet a room when she entered. The images of Jesus in the paintings on the walls of our Sunday school class had Him looking like a gentle rock star, or perhaps somebody who played folk music and rarely talked, just strummed on his guitar and occasionally swiped his hair back behind his ear. It confused me later when I read His grim physical description in Scripture. Here is a description of Jesus in the book of Isaiah:

> He had no beauty or majesty to attract us to him, nothing in his appearance that we should desire him. He was despised and rejected by men, a man of sorrows, and familiar with suffering. Like one from whom men hide their faces he was despised, and we esteemed him not. (53:2–3 NIV)

I realize this isn't a lot to go on, but it is enough for us to know He wasn't exactly Brad Pitt. It seems odd to me that God would want us to know Jesus was unsightly. It was as though the way Christ looked was part of the message He was to communicate.

I watched an interview with Mel Gibson recently about his film *The Passion of the Christ.* Gibson said it was important for Jesus to look very masculine in the film, and he wanted an actor who was good-looking. And I thought the movie *The Passion* was quite beautiful, but I wondered if very many people would go to see it if the guy who played Jesus in the movie were ugly. And that made me wonder how many people would follow Jesus today if, say, He showed up in America looking the way He looked thousands of years ago. I wondered if anybody would want to interview Jesus on television. I'll bet, if Jesus came to America and tried to do television interviews, the only people who would interview Him would be the people on public television, because on public television, they are not concerned about associating their television personalities with the commercial endorsement of products.

I read a report in the *Journal of Applied Social Psychology* that said criminals perceived as handsome were given lighter sentences than those perceived as unattractive. The article said researchers in

Pennsylvania studied photographs of seventy-four defendants, judging them regarding their attractiveness, and the trials of the seventy-four revealed that men judged less handsome were twice as likely to be sent to jail as attractive men, who were handed significantly lighter sentences when convicted. In the lifeboat, Jesus was definitely representing humanity as equal, hardly caring about how He looked. One might believe that the unsightliness of Christ was a statement of humility, but this isn't true. It would be inconsistent if Christ's looks were a statement of humility. They were, rather, a statement of truth, and our seeing them as humility only suggests an obvious prejudice.

He Liked to Be with People

My friend Jared told me recently about a friend of his who works at a restaurant in Aspen, Colorado. His friend is a fan of former President Bill Clinton, who on two occasions visited the restaurant in which he worked. He said the first time the president came in they struck up a conversation over a beer, the president sitting quietly and listening to the stories this waiter told about living in the area and working at the restaurant. About a year later, the president was visiting Aspen again and went into the same restaurant, walked up to the waiter, and called him by name. One of the most powerful men in the world remembered a waiter's name a year after meeting him.

I realize most evangelicals don't like the former president for his policies and moral shortcomings, but the story has always fascinated me, and even when I see Bill Clinton on television I get the feeling he would like me were we to sit down together and talk. We do not know whether President Clinton really likes people or if his altruism is politically motivated. I tend to think he actually likes people. Regardless, it is a rare person who gets this much life from being around people. It is a rare person who loses himself in the presence of other human beings.

Perhaps the most comforting characteristic of Christ is that He liked people. Were somebody to ask me to begin a religious system, I would sit down and write a book the way Muhammad and Joseph Smith both did. This would seem the most logical way to communicate new ideas. Writing in scrolls, however, was not something that interested Jesus. He never sat down and wrote a mission statement. Instead, He accumulated friends and allowed them to write about Him, talk about Him, testify about Him. Each of the Gospels reveals a Christ who ate with people, attended parties, drank with people, prayed with people, traveled with people, and worked with people. I can't imagine He would do this unless He actually liked people and cared about them. Jesus built our faith system entirely on relationships, forgoing marketing efforts and spin.

Not only that, but one of the criticisms of Christ was that He was a friend of pagans. Not that He hung out with pagans, but that He was their friend.

I take great comfort in the possibility that Jesus would like me were we to meet face-to-face. To be sure, there were people Jesus did not take a liking to, but those people were arrogant, questioned His identity as God, and boosted their egos and senses of power by burdening people with excess religious baggage. But for most people, especially people in the margins, there was in Christ a great deal of empathy. He seemed to want people to be together, to live together and love one another and link arms. In John 17:21–23, Christ prays that those of us who hear His gospel through the work of the disciples would be one, just as He and the Father are One. And when asked what is the greatest commandment, Jesus replies that it is *to love the Father*, a relational exploit, and He adds, as if to emphasize, *to love as well our neighbors* (see Matt. 22:36–39). Christ is saying that the two most important commandments of God are to have within us a relational commitment to God and to other people. This isn't even to mention the fact that, as God, He created people in the first place. God calls us His children, His sheep, and His bride.

It must have been wonderful to spend time with Christ, with Somebody who liked you, loved you, believed in you, and sought a closeness foreign to skin-bound man. A person would feel significant in His presence. After all, those who knew Christ personally went on to accomplish amazing feats, proving unwavering devotion. It must have been thrilling to look into the eyes of God and have Him look back and communicate that human beings, down to the individual, are of immense worth and beauty and worthy of intimacy with each other and the Godhead. Such an understanding fueled a lifetime of joy and emotional health among the disciples that neither crowds of people jeering insults nor prison nor torture nor exclusion could undo. They were faithful to the end, even to their own deaths.

People don't go out and get tortured and arrested for somebody who doesn't love them. If somebody loves us we will do all kinds of things in their name, for them, because of them. They will make us who we are.

I recently read an interview in which the Nobel Prize–winning novelist Toni Morrison was asked why she had become a great writer, what books she had read, what method she had used to structure her practice. She laughed and said, "Oh, no, that is not why I am a great writer. I am a great writer because when I was a little girl and walked into a room where my father was sitting, his eyes would light up. That is why I am a great writer. That is why. There isn't any other reason."

Imagine these guys knowing, for a fact, that God in heaven, their Father, the Creator of all the cosmos, loved them. When I read about what happened to Stephen, Peter, Paul, and the rest of the disciples, I know for a fact that Christ expressed immense love for them. I know in my heart that they were not living the lives they lived or dying the deaths they died because they were doing something "right." Sure it was right, but these guys must have been loved by Christ, and their motivation came primarily from this idea. There is no other explanation for their devotion.

And I kept wondering about the people who met Christ who were losers in the lifeboat, the crippled and the blind, the woman at the well, Mary Magdalene, and Zacchaeus. Entire communities had shunned them and told them they were no good, but God, the King of the universe, comes walking down the street and looks them in the eye, holds their hands, embraces them, eats at their tables, in their homes, for all the town to see. That must have been the greatest moment of their lives.

It is true that it is a powerful occurrence to have somebody look you in the eye and say you are worth something. I was reading an issue of *Smithsonian* magazine the other day and in it was an interview with the poet Maya Angelou. In the interview she talked about the time, as only an eight-year-old girl, that she was raped by her mother's boyfriend. She spoke about having to heal from the crime, but also about how she told on the man, and how he had gone to prison and, shortly after being released, was beaten to death by men in the community. Angelou believes she was the one who caused the man's death because she told about the rape. I was amazed to read that after the beating, the terrified young child didn't speak for years. It was much later, during a walk with her mother, that she would find the source of her life of freedom, beauty, and creativity. Walking down a street near their home, Angelou said her mother stopped, turned, and spoke to her:

"Baby," she said, looking the young woman in the eye. "You know something? I think you are the greatest woman I have ever met. Yes. Mary McLeod Bethune, Eleanor Roosevelt, my mother, and you—and you are the greatest." Maya Angelou said in the interview that she boarded a streetcar with tears flowing down her cheeks, stared into the wood paneling of the car and thought to herself, *Suppose I really am somebody?*

And yes, she was and is somebody. On the bulletin board above my desk, I have a picture of Angelou in which she is delivering a poem at President Clinton's inauguration. Far from the girl who spent years living in fear and silence, the brilliant poet stood before the nation and spoke compellingly:

> But today, the Rock cries out to us,
> clearly, forcefully,
> Come, you may stand upon my
> Back and face your distant destiny!

I love the line "the Rock cries out to us." I think that is beautiful, for some reason, maybe because Jesus was like Maya Angelou's mother in that He went around looking people in the eye to tell them they were beautiful, that He stood as a rock for them, a Being who, for the rest of their lives, they could look back to and hear in their minds and envision in their memories, God saying to them the world had been lying, and you are indeed beautiful.

Last year I pulled a friend out of his closet. He was drunk and his wife was pacing the house in tears, unable to find him. His marriage was falling apart because of his inability to stop drinking.

This man is a kind and brilliant human being, touched with many gifts from God, but addicted to alcohol, and being taken down in the fight. He was suicidal, we thought, and the kids had been sent away. We sat together on his back deck and talked for hours, deep into the night. I didn't think he was going to make it. I worried about him as I boarded my flight back to Portland and he checked himself into rehab.

Two months later he picked me up from the same airport, having gone several weeks without a drink. As he told me the story of the beginnings of his painful recovery process, he said a single incident was giving him the strength to continue. His father had flown in to attend a recovery meeting with him, and in the meeting my friend had to confess all his issues and weaknesses. When he finished, his father stood up to address the group of addicts. He looked to his son and said, "I have never loved my son as much as I do at this moment. I love him. I want all of you to know I love him." My friend said at that moment, for the first time in his life, he was able to believe God loved him, too. He believed if God, his father, and his wife all loved him, he could fight the addiction, and he believed he might make it.

I often reflect about the author of the gospel of John and wonder if he did not receive as much from Christ as my friend did that day from his father. *I am the one Jesus loved*, John would say of himself in his account of the life of Christ.

The essence of Christ's ministry was to display the worth of humanity, all stemming from God's love for them. Even today, as Christ works to minister to hurting people through His servants, the message is the same.

A few years ago I sat down with a man named Ron Post. Ron was about to retire from a ministry he had started twenty years before called Northwest Medical Teams. Northwest Medical Teams is an aid organization that sends doctors to volatile regions of the world to help the sick and dying. We met at a coffee shop across town, and I asked Ron questions about how he had built this eighty-million-dollars-per-year ministry, with 98 percent of the money going directly to the work being done in the field. I asked him how he structured his time, how he delegated responsibility, and finally asked him what was the key to his success. To answer the last question, Ron pulled from his pocket a tattered envelope filled with pictures.

For the rest of the meeting the man laid down pictures of people he had met, the first of whom was a young Cambodian woman who, at the age of thirteen, was being used as a sex slave to the Khmer Rouge. He told me they had rescued her from captivity and given her a new life filled with the knowledge and love of Christ. As he showed me picture after picture of blind people who, because of a simple surgery, could now see, crippled people who could walk, the starving who had been fed, he told me their names. *He knew their names, every one of them.* I had asked the man what the key to his successful ministry was, and he told me through his stories the key to his multimillion-dollar ministry was a love of people. And I believe now and will always believe that if we are willing to love people, God will pour out His resources to bless our lives and our efforts.

I think of this meeting with Ron when I consider Christ, who, like Ron, must have a proverbial envelope in His pocket, laying down picture after picture, knowing our names, knowing the number of hairs that grow on our heads, knowing our stories and fears and desires. He looks at each of us and feels in His heart the kind of love that would make Him want to come to earth and die so we could be healed, so we could feel the love that is going to make us whole, that is going to rescue us from the lifeboat.

He Had No Fear of Intimacy

I have sometimes wondered if the greatest desire of man is to be known and loved anyway. It is no secret we are terribly protective of our hearts, as though this tender space is a kind of receptor for our validation as humans. The closer we are to another person, the more vulnerable we are and the more we feel a sense of risk. Lovers can take years to finally trust each other, and many of us will close ourselves off at the slightest hint of danger. Introductory conversations are almost always shallow. "Where did you go to school?" and "How old are your children?" are safe places to begin. Start an initial meeting with "What addictions do you struggle with?" or "When do you feel least loved by your wife?" and we are going to have a tough time making new friends. It seems that we feel we must trust people before we let them know anything remotely vulnerable about us, and to ask for more before trust has been built is to contravene a social etiquette dating back to the fall of man. All this, I suppose, is connected to the fact that our validation seems to always be in question.

And yet it is through this system of defense that Christ walks with ease, never seeming to fear that He would do damage by rummaging around in the tender complexity of a person's identity. Instead, He goes nearly immediately to our greatest fears, our most injured spaces, and speaks into those places with authority.

John includes in his gospel an interaction between Jesus and a woman from Samaria. She was from a group of people known in the day for subscribing to loose interpretation of the Judaic system; the modern-day, evangelical equivalent of a Unitarian. In the scene, Jesus is alone with this woman at a well, where He has come for a drink and she has come to draw water for the day. The woman has a loose reputation, according to the text, having gone through five husbands. In this day, it was nearly unheard of for Jews to have any dealings at all with Samaritans, much less women of her repute. The woman is shocked when Jesus asks her for a drink of water. "How is it that You, being a Jew, ask a drink from me, a Samaritan woman?" she says to Jesus (John 4:9 NKJV).

A friend recently told me that this exchange would be the equivalent of a known evangelical walking into a gay bar and asking a man to buy him a beer.

"Listen," Christ says to the woman. "If you knew the gift of God, and who it is who says to you, 'Give Me a drink,' you would have asked Him, and He would have given you living water" (v. 10).

This odd response must have frustrated the woman, because she responds sarcastically, "I would like to have some of that water because I wouldn't have to keep coming out here to this well!" (see v. 15).

And then Christ walks directly past the barriers around this woman's heart as if He had been destined to live in and warm those cold chambers. "Go, call your husband, and come here," He says to her (v. 16).

The text indicates Christ knows full well the woman has had five husbands and is now living with a man to whom she is not married. The interesting nature of Christ's words is that they correct a misunderstanding. The woman had assumed the living water Christ talked about was like the liquid in the well, but instead, Christ redirects her immediately to a thirst of a different sort: this desire to be known and loved anyway. In no way does Jesus judge this woman, stand over her and condemn her, or even mention the idea of sin; rather, He appeals to the desire of her heart, pointing out the dehumanizing cycle of her life that has driven her through relationship after relationship, none of which gave her lasting fulfillment. In a sense, this woman was looking for importance and love through a man, and Jesus walks up and says what you really need is God, what I have is living water; and if you drink of it, you will never thirst again. It is interesting to me that He offers Himself to the deepest need of man, not a religion, not a formula, but Himself. He offers to her a relationship that is more than romantic, more than a balm for her heart. "I know that Messiah is coming," she says to Jesus. "I who speak to you am He," Christ responds (vv. 25–26).

It must have been unnerving when, to an elitist audience, Jesus later would tell a parable about a man who had been robbed and beaten and then ignored by all but a "good Samaritan." Jesus was not afraid of controversy, of revealing the worth of those considered worthless. The modern-day equivalent might be to tell a story to a group of conservative evangelicals about a pluralist, liberal homosexual who heroically stops to help a stranded traveler after a preacher, a Republican, and a Christian writer have passed him by.

He Was Patient

My pastor and friend Rick McKinley talked to me recently about a meeting he had with a young pastor who was beginning a church plant in another city. In the course of the conversation, the young pastor asked Rick at what point he should kick people out of leadership because they were failing to understand the nature of ministry. Rick looked at the pastor, confused. "Kick them out of leadership?" Rick asked. "Sure," the young pastor replied. "We have to move forward, right? And if they don't get it, I need to weed them out."

Rick sat back and laughed. "Listen," he said. "If I'd thrown out the guys who didn't get it when I started Imago, we wouldn't have anybody left, including me! You are never going to build a church by kicking people out. This isn't a fast-food restaurant; it's the kingdom of God, and quality disciples take a lot of time. Jesus is patient to the end."

It occurred to me as I read through the Gospels that Rick got his patience with people directly from Christ. It took Jesus years to develop the disciples into community-oriented guys. Years into their relationship with Christ, after hearing Him teach perhaps hundreds of times, the disciples were still asking questions like "Who of us is going to be the most important in heaven?" (see Mark 9:34). In a sense, they were asking Jesus who was more important in the lifeboat, and the whole time, Jesus had been teaching them that the lifeboat feelings were worthless. If this were a corporation, these guys would have been let go.

In the last chapter of his gospel, John shows the unending nature of Christ's patience with people. Jesus has risen from the dead and already revealed Himself to the disciples, and yet some of them, including Peter, have gone fishing. Jesus searches out these guys and finds them fishing. They don't recognize Him on the distant shore, and so the Lord calls to them and asks if they have had any success fishing. "No," they reply, and so Christ tells them to cast their net on the other side of the boat. The disciples do this and find so many fish they can't pull the net into the boat. (See John 21:1–6.) This is the same miracle Christ performed when He first met Peter, asking him to follow Him, telling Peter He would make him a fisher of men (see Matthew 4:18–19).

My friend David Gentiles observes a few interesting dynamics in this scene. The first idea is that Peter had spent the last three years traveling with Christ, watching miracles be performed, listening to Jesus' proclamations about His Godhead, and noting the many prophecies that were being fulfilled daily, and yet after all of this, he is back where Jesus had found him: fishing. The second observation is the number of times John mentions the actual presence of fish. John says they were fishing, John gives the exact number of fish they caught, John says the fish were dragged onto the shore where they were sitting, John says Christ made a fire and cooked them breakfast, leading us to assume they were eating fish. (See John 21:1–13.)

John then goes into detail about a conversation Jesus had with Peter. In the conversation Jesus says to Peter, "Do you love Me more than these?" (21:15 NKJV). David Gentiles wonders if Christ is talking not about the other disciples, as I first thought when I read the text, but rather about the fish. After all, John isn't a writer who wastes words, and he did bring up the fish several times, hardly mentioning the other disciples.

You can imagine the surprise in Peter's response when he says: "You know all things; You know that I love You" (21:17 NKJV). Not once but three times Jesus comes back and asks Peter if he loves Him more than these fish. And each time Peter responds emphatically yes, he does. And Jesus continues to tell Peter that if he loves Him, he will feed His sheep, which most scholars agree means Peter will help build the church. It goes without saying that most people trying to change a faith system the way Christ was doing would have let Peter go a long time before this, but to the end Jesus is showing patience with Peter, believing in Peter and helping Peter understand the nature of this new kind of redemption.

Historical accounts of the death of Peter suggest he got it. Catholic history books portray Peter as brave to the last, being dragged off toward his cross, appealing to his wife, who was also going to be crucified, to remember the Lord.

This comforts me because I know how very long it has taken me to trust completely in Christ and to understand the ramifications of my relationship with Him. I read this text feeling gratitude that Jesus has patience with me, that He wants me to understand and He isn't going to give up on me any time soon.

He Was Kind

I read a quotation recently in which the French emperor Napoleon Bonaparte, musing on the negotiation of clout, gave an appropriate summation of the power of Christ's love and kindness, saying, "I know men; and I tell you that Jesus Christ is no mere man. Between Him and every other person in the world there is no possible term of comparison. Alexander, Caesar, Charlemagne, and I have founded empires. But on what did we rest the creations of our genius? Upon force! Jesus Christ founded His empire upon love; and at this hour millions of men would die for Him."

I confess, I have often wondered how a soft Jesus would instill such devotion in the hearts of men. I suppose the answer rests in this mingling of challenge and kindness. But the kindness part is not so palatable for me, the word *kindness* rings as a synonym to, well, *weakness, wimpiness.*

I came across a book a few years ago, however, that helped me understand the power of kindness in leadership. The book was about a man named John Gagliardi and his career as head football coach at St. John's University. The unorthodox method in which Coach Gagliardi leads his players is intriguing, if not completely odd. An anomaly to say the least, Coach Gagliardi does not ask his players to lift weights during the off-season, holds no spring practice, and rarely allows players to hit each other during drills. Instead, Gagliardi employs an exercise called the "Nice Day Drill" in which players lie flat on their backs, stretch left and say to the player beside them, *Nice day,* then stretch right to say the same to the player on the other side. During stretching exercises, captains greet their teams with smiles and ask them to comment on the beauty of the day. Players then look around the field, up to the sky, out to the trees, and comment on the nice colors and soft breezes.

I couldn't help but laugh as I read, quite honestly, until I got to the part of the book that mentions St. John's win record within their very competitive division. Coach Gagliardi is the winningest football coach in the history of college football or, for that matter, any football. He has more wins than any five NFL coaches combined. The results of Gagliardi's unique philosophy are phenomenal. And what of the performance on the field? The players systematically score above each and every rival, recently by more than 70 points.

John Gagliardi points out that St. John's is a Catholic school and the monks who run the university, when they hired him, were looking for two things in their football program: (1) a program that reflected the leadership style of Jesus, and (2) wins. Lots and lots of wins.

Coach Gagliardi says players are asked to treat their teammates in the way they would like to be treated, with kindness, graciousness, and altruism. The players work as hard as they want to work, and when they come to practice they do exactly as the coach asks them to do, not because their positions will be threatened if they don't (St. John's offers no football scholarships), but because they care about one another, work as a team, and love their coach because they sense his love for them.

And so when I consider the way I am treated by Christ, the degree of kindness with which He guides me, I know that as Napoleon said, I would die for Him. And I would not die for Him because He threatens me; I would die for Him because He loves me, and because I am part of a community of people who are committed to one another, to the world, and to the mission of Jesus.

I suspect this was a great draw for those who chose to follow

Christ. I suspect the degree of community and camaraderie embodied by the initial Twelve was as appealing as food for the starving soul. The religious leadership of the day tended to be overbearing, unkind, and exclusionary, no doubt leaving those who encountered them with a feeling of worthlessness. The religious leaders of the day were against people who were not like them, and Jesus' sincere appreciation of human beings must have been a welcome contrast.

The emotional needs of those around Him were only a portion of Jesus' concerns. He was no less aware of tangible needs. In a scene captured by Mark, Jesus becomes uneasy that the thousands who have come to hear His proclamations will not be able to get back home before they need dinner. In one of the more dramatic of His miracles, Jesus takes a small ration of food and divides it for as many as ten thousand people, creating enough food for every person in the crowd to eat until they are full. (See Mark 8:2–9, noting that only men are accounted for.) The fact that each man, woman, and child was fed to satisfaction struck me as an indication of Christ's awareness, empathy, and kindness for humanity.

Questioned by Pharisees about His willingness to perform miracles on the Sabbath, a day on which no work was to be done, Jesus asked His indicters if they would be willing to aid one of their animals were it to have fallen into a ravine. "Certainly," His accusers answered Him. "Surely kindness to people is as legal as kindness to animals!" Christ responded, perhaps challenging the merit of His questioners' philosophy on the basis of their humanitarian failures. (See Matthew 12:9–12.)

He Was God

Many people were convinced Jesus was God even when He was still a baby. I say this only because He wasn't the guy who went around telling people He was God when He was thirty. He did that, but a lot of people thought He was God well before on account of some angels appeared to some shepherds, and some wise men got word of His birth and traveled a long way to see Him. King Herod even heard about Jesus being born and decided to kill all the young children in Israel because he was worried that Jesus was going to grow up and threaten his throne. If you consider these ideas, you had blue-collar guys thinking Jesus was God, you had wise men from different countries thinking He was God, you had King Herod thinking He was a King; and I know that doesn't prove anything, but if He were just some kind of freak going around saying He was God, He wouldn't have had all those people running around saying He was God even while He was a baby. These days you get guys who say they are God, and the only people who believe them are the ones who are brainwashed by them in the first place. And even then the guys who say they are God always want to sleep with everybody's wife and live on an island and drink a lot of punch and drive expensive cars and do crazy stuff that pretty much proves they aren't God.

When Jesus was a baby a man named Simeon was visited by an angel and told that he would see the Messiah before he died, and later, after Jesus was born, Simeon walked into the temple, took Jesus into his arms, and said, "Lord, now You are letting Your servant depart in peace, according to Your word; for my eyes have seen Your salvation which You have prepared before the face of all peoples, a light to bring revelation to the Gentiles, and the glory of Your people Israel" (Luke 2:29–32 NKJV).

These kinds of prophecies help me believe Jesus was the actual Son of God and God Himself. And it makes you wonder what Joseph and Mary thought about all this. Both of them had already been visited by angels who told them this kid was going to be special; but having guys pick up your baby and say He was God, that He was going to deliver salvation to the world, would be confusing to say the least. The gospel of Luke even comments that Joseph and Mary were amazed at the things being said about their son (2:33), which I take to mean they didn't fully understand what was happening or who, exactly, Jesus was.

It's true there were a lot of false messiahs at the time. Many of the Jews were looking for Him to come at any time, so a lot of people were pretending to be the guy, either because the devil had put them up to it or because they wanted attention, but none of them were being picked up as a baby and told they were going to be the salvation of the world, and none of them were being visited by shepherds and wise men, and none of them were causing kings to panic so badly they killed an entire generation of small children. These things are unique to the birth of Christ.

But the stuff that helps me believe Jesus was actually God is really the social stuff, the stuff about how He contradicted the lifeboat thinking you and I live within. If the guy was actually God, and the Trinity worked the way the Bible says the Trinity worked, and if man really was wired to work right only in the company of God, and if God left, and then if God came down here to save us, Jesus would pretty much be the personality we'd expect God to have, and the way the world would have reacted to Him would be pretty much the way the world reacted to Him. It's quite remarkable, if you think about it. The personality of Jesus fits right into the whole of the story. But if a person were to need more proof than this, as many people do, there are a lot of prophecies fulfilled by Jesus that set Him apart from the false messiahs.

Simeon, while holding Christ as a baby, is one of the last prophets to foretell the coming Messiah. An eerie litany of prophets laid themselves out in the centuries before Christ as a sign for the

Jews that Jesus was coming. Each of these prophets foretold events in Christ's life including but not limited to His genealogy, His persecution, and His death. The Messiah had been spelled out as coming from the seed of woman (Gen. 3:15), a descendant of Abraham (Gen. 12:3), a descendant of Isaac (Gen. 17:19), a descendant of Jacob (Num. 24:17), from the tribe of Judah (Gen. 49:10), heir to the throne of David (Isa. 9:7), to be born in Bethlehem (Mic. 5:2), to be born of a virgin (Isa. 7:14), to flee to Egypt (Hos. 11:1), to be preceded by a forerunner (Mal. 3:1), to minister in Galilee (Isa. 9:1), to speak in parables (Ps. 78:2–4), to bind up the brokenhearted (Isa. 61:1), to be rejected by the Jews (Isa. 53:3), to enter Jerusalem triumphantly (Zech. 9:9), adored by infants (Ps. 8:2), betrayed by a dear friend (Ps. 41:9), betrayed for thirty pieces of silver (Zech. 11:12), silent to accusations (Isa. 53:7), spat on and struck (Isa. 50:6), to serve as a vicarious sacrifice (Isa. 53:5), to be crucified with criminals (Isa. 53:12), to be pierced through the hands and feet (Zech. 12:10), to be sneered at and mocked (Ps. 22:7), to have His clothes distributed by gamblers (Ps. 22:18), to be forsaken by God (Ps. 22:1), to be killed bones intact (Ps. 34:20), to be pierced in the side (Zech. 12:10), and buried with the rich (Isa. 53:9), to be resurrected (Pss. 16:10; 49:15), and to ascend to God's right hand (Ps. 68:18).

And if you consider all of these prophecies, it is a pretty tough list to fulfill. It would take a lot of work to get all that done, much of it, such as being preceded by John the Baptist, fleeing to Egypt, being killed by crucifixion and yet not having a bone broken, being recognized as a baby, and rising from the dead is stuff you can't control unless you are, in fact, God.

Still, I think the reason religious people rejected Jesus was because His fulfillment of the prophecies didn't look the way they expected them to look. They wanted Jesus to come down and be this very respectable type in an earthly way, rich and good-looking and all, only so He would make their religious system look good, only so He would make *them* look good. What they wanted was for God to come down and redeem them to a jury of their peers, not a God who came down to care about the poor and sick and contradict the lifeboat economy altogether. Back then, it was best to look a certain way and talk a certain way and act a certain way in order to make the religion look good, and Jesus pretty much smashed all that to pieces. This was great trouble for people who were in the business of running a public relations campaign for God.

I must admit, while at first critical of religious leaders for rejecting Christ, I began to wonder what it might feel like if Jesus came back today, you know, right in the middle of America, right in the middle of our church culture. I imagined the second coming of Jesus as prophesied in various Scriptures of the New Testament. The prophecies aimed at us about the Second Coming have Jesus showing up like a thief in the night, returning as trumpets sound, and riding a horse. When I imagine this, my mind has Jesus riding through the clouds, very suddenly and to much ado, the entire world trembling at His return, all people awakened from their sleep, acknowledging the King of the universe.

But what if the guys playing the horns turned out to be a few men playing on a street corner in a small town in Arkansas, and what if the horse Jesus rode in on wasn't a Kentucky thoroughbred, but a belligerent donkey? And what if Jesus, after He got here, frequented homeless shelters and bars and ate and drank with the kinds of cultures evangelicals have declared war against? And what if, when He came like a thief in the night, He came very quietly so that nobody noticed, and what if, crime of all crimes, He was ugly and when He went on CNN producers were uncomfortable with His appearance and only shot Him from the waist up, in a certain light? And what if, when He answered questions, He talked with a hick accent, and only spoke in parables that nobody could understand, and what if He didn't align Himself with a political party, and what if He didn't kiss anybody's butt?

If you ask me, He'd have to do a lot of miracles to overcome all that stuff. And even then, most of the people who would follow Him would be people who were oppressed, marginalized, and desperate.

Jewish leaders mocked Jesus for His having come from Nazareth and claiming to be the Messiah and for His association with drunkards and gluttons, for His refusal to bow down to the powers that be, and for disregarding Jewish customs. Yes, the prophecies were fulfilled, but not in the way the Jews had anticipated.

And so, as prophesied by Isaiah, Jesus was rejected by the people God had preserved (see Isaiah 53:3). Jewish culture had established a hierarchy of power as well as an economy associated with their religious system. If God were going to step out of heaven, end the existing redemptive system, and disrupt the power structure and financial organism that sustained them, He'd need to do it with a bit more flare.

Here is how John the Evangelist captures part of the rejection: "I give them eternal life, and they shall never perish," Jesus begins. "No one can snatch them out of my hand. My Father, who has given them to me, is greater than all; no one can snatch them out of my Father's hand. I and the Father are one" (John 10:28–30 NIV).

At this point the Jews picked up stones to try to kill Him.

"I have shown you many great miracles from the Father," Jesus said to them. "For which of these do you stone me?"

"We are not stoning you for any of these," replied the Jews, "but for blasphemy, because you, a mere man, claim to be God" (vv. 31–33 NIV).

—

Sometimes I think it is easier for you and me to believe Jesus is God now that He is in heaven than it might have been back when He was walking around on earth. If you had seen Jesus do miracles, and if you were one of those who were healed by Him or one of the disciples, then it would have been easier, but for most people, especially the Jews, Jesus would have been a stumbling block.

At the same time, however, we are at a disadvantage because the Jesus that exists in our minds is hardly the real Jesus. The Jesus on CNN, the Jesus in our books and in our movies, the Jesus that is a collection of evangelical personalities, is often a Jesus of the suburbs, a Jesus who wants you to be a better yuppie, a Jesus who is extremely political and supports a specific party, a Jesus who has declared a kind of culture war in the name of our children, a Jesus who worked through the founding fathers to begin America, a Jesus who dresses very well, speaks perfect English, has three points that fulfill any number of promises, and wants you and me to be, above all, comfortable. Is this the real Jesus?

Is Jesus sitting in the lifeboat with us, stroking our backs and telling us we are the ones who are right and one day these other infidels are going to pay, that we are the ones who are going to survive and the others are going to be thrown over because we are Calvinists, Armenians, Baptists, Methodists, Catholics; because we are Republicans, Democrats, conservatives, liberals; because we attend a big church, a small church, an ethnically diverse church, a house church; or is Jesus acting in our hearts to reach out to the person who isn't like us—the oppressed, the poor, the unchurched—and to humble ourselves, give of our money, build our communities in love, give our time and our creativity, get on our knees before our enemies in humility, treating them as Scripture says, as people who are more important than we are? The latter is the Jesus of Scripture; the former, which is infinitely more popular in evangelical culture, is a myth sharing a genre with unicorns.

He Is I AM

And even as I have attempted to explain the personality of Christ in an effort to give us a better look at who God is, I fear I haven't come close. John said all the books in the world couldn't contain the works Jesus did while He was on earth (see John 21:25). There is so much more, so much that can't be explained, so much more than our minds could possibly understand. It makes me wonder at the difficulty God Himself had in explaining His nature to His own creation.

In an exchange recorded in the book of Exodus, God is speaking to Moses through a burning bush. Moses asks God a seemingly adolescent question, knowing full well he is speaking with God: "Who should I say sent me?"

Moses might well have been asking, *How do I explain You? What is Your identity?* And within God's answer to the question we feel the limitations of language. God simply answers: "I AM WHO I AM."

The Jews would know well this encounter between Moses and God, and it would have undoubtedly come to mind when Jesus answered His inquisitors' similar question by repeating the phrase "I AM." And yet it is a fitting reply for a Creator explaining Himself to His creation. God did not answer, "I EXIST," or offer one of His names, all of which are metaphors invented for humans, but rather, "I AM." Climbing inside letters, God explains, *I encompass, I am beyond existence, I am nothing you will understand, I have no beginning and no end, I am not like you, and yet I AM.*

Christmas has just passed here in Portland. It is New Year's Day, and I am seated by my upstairs window watching snow gather on the roads and frost the stick limbs of trees. It snows here once every few years, and yet rarely as early in winter as Christmas. It was a busy season for me. Prior engagements had me spending Christmas in town, unable to fly to my family. I spent Christmas Eve and Christmas Day seated at my computer writing this chapter; all words about Jesus. My affection for Him has grown so much over the years there were times I confess, as I wrote, I had to shut down the computer because I felt the text was getting mushy. It is not difficult for me to believe Jesus liked people, or that He was different from the religious establishment who represented strict, stoic spirituality of the day; it is not difficult for me to believe He loves you, or my wealthy neighbors, or the people I ride the bus with every day. His personality would have to have been dynamic and filled with love to shift a religious system as great as Judaism into a system as tiny and understated as Christianity.

This business of His being God, however, is another idea entirely. I cannot understand it. Of course I believe, but I confess, when I think of Jesus I do not think of Him in His preheavenly state, some great existence beyond existence, some great I AM; rather, I see Him in a manger, I see Him building a house, I see Him walking among the poor or standing in the synagogues, which is a state He encompassed for a span of time the Bible refers to as only a vapor. Jesus as God? Could a mind process such an idea, and does belief require understanding? I don't suspect it does, for I believe and yet do not understand.

And yet, to a spiritual community that offers formula in place of faith, a belief that Jesus was the Son of God and God as well is more than a description of the Messenger of the gospel, it is entwined in the message itself, and the idea seems as necessary as the words He speaks. There is no question that a part of what we believe as Christians is that Jesus was in fact God. We cling to this as truth, we cling to that which we do not understand, just as love causes a man to cling to a woman, and love causes a father or mother to connect deeply with his or her child. Indeed, as Jesus looks across the social landscape into the fear-filled eyes of the inhabitants of the lifeboat, He does not offer a formula that will help us win the game, He offers Himself.

I want to tell you without reservation that if there is any hope for you and me, for this planet set off-kilter in the fifteen-billion light-year expanse of endless mystery, the hope would have to be in this Man who contends He is not of us, but with us, and simply IS. I AM WHO I AM.

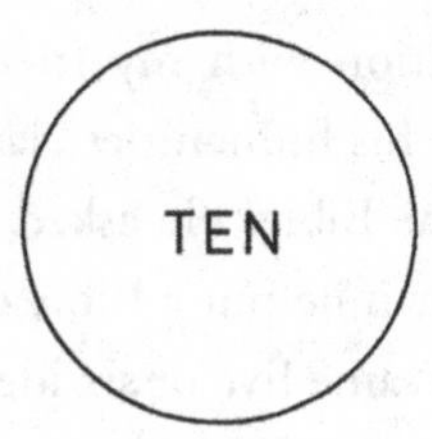

TEN

The Gospel of Jesus

It Never Was a Formula

My friend Greg and I have been talking quite a bit about what it means to follow Jesus. Greg would not consider himself as somebody who takes Jesus seriously, but he admits to having questions. I didn't have a formula for him to understand how a Christian conversion works, but I told him that many years ago, when I was a child, I had heard about Jesus and found the idea of Him compelling, then much later, while reading the Gospels, came to believe I wanted to follow Him. This changed things in my life, I said, because it involved giving up everything and choosing to go into a relationship with Him.

Greg told me he had seen a pamphlet with four or five ideas on it, ideas such as man was a sinner, sin separated man from God, and Christ died to absolve the separation. He asked me if this was what I believed, and I told him, essentially, that it was. "Those would be the facts of the story," I said, "but that isn't the story."

"Those are the ideas, but it isn't the narrative," Greg stated rhetorically.

"Yes," I told him.

Earlier that same year I had a conversation with my friend Omar, who is a student at a local college. For his humanities class, Omar was assigned to read the majority of the Bible. He asked to meet with me for coffee, and when we sat down he put a Bible on the table as well as a pamphlet containing the same five or six ideas Greg had mentioned. He opened the pamphlet, read the ideas, and asked if these concepts were important to the central message of Christianity. I told Omar they were critical; that, basically, this was the gospel of Jesus, the backbone of Christian faith. Omar then opened his Bible and asked, "If these ideas are so important, why aren't they in this book?"

"But the Scripture references are right here," I said curiously, showing Omar that the verses were printed next to each idea.

"I see that," he said. "But in the Bible they aren't concise like they are in this pamphlet. They are spread out all over the book."

"But this pamphlet is a summation of the ideas," I clarified.

"Right," Omar continued, "but it seems like, if these ideas are that critical, God would have taken the time to make bullet points out of them. Instead, He put some of them here and some of them there. And half the time, when Jesus is talking, He is speaking entirely in parables. It is hard to believe that whatever it is He is talking about can be summed up this simply."

Omar's point is well taken. And while the ideas presented in these pamphlets are certainly true, it struck me how simply we had begun to explain the ideas, not only how simply, but how non-relationally, how propositionally. I don't mean any of this to fault the pamphlets at all. Tracts such as the ones Omar and Greg encountered have been powerful tools in helping people understand the beauty of the message of Christ. Millions, perhaps, have come to know Jesus through these efficient presentations of the gospel. But I did begin to wonder if there were better ways of explaining it than these pamphlets. After all, the pamphlets have been around for only the last fifty years or so (along with our formulaic presentation of the gospel), and the church has shrunk, not grown, in Western countries in which these tools have been used. But the greater trouble with these reduced ideas is that modern evangelical culture is so accustomed to this summation that it is difficult for us to see the gospel as anything other than a list of true statements with which a person must agree.

It makes me wonder if, because of this reduced version of the claims of Christ, we believe the gospel is easy to understand, a simple mental exercise, not the least bit mysterious. And if you think about it, a person has a more difficult time explaining romantic love, for instance, or beauty, or the Trinity, than the gospel of Jesus. John would open his gospel by presenting the idea that God is the Word and Jesus is the Word and the Word became flesh and dwelt among us. Not exactly bullet points for easy consumption. Perhaps our reduction of these ideas has caused us to miss something.

—

Each year I teach a class on the gospel and culture at a small Bible college back East. This year I asked the students to list the precepts a person would need to understand in order to become a Christian. I stood at the whiteboard and they called out ideas: Man was sinful by nature; sin separates us from God; Jesus died for our sins; we could accept Jesus into our hearts (after some thought, students were not able to explain exactly what they meant by this, only saying it was a kind of interaction in which a person agrees Jesus is the Son of God), and so on. Then, looking at the board, I began to ask some questions about these almost universally accepted ideas. I asked if a person could believe all these ideas were true and yet not be a Christian. I told them my friend Matt, for instance, believed all these ideas and yet would never claim to be a person who knows Jesus or much less follows Him. The students conceded that, in fact, a person could know and even believe all the concepts on the board and yet not be a Christian. "Then there is something missing, isn't there?" I said to the class. "It isn't watertight just yet. There must be some idea we are leaving out, some fool-proof thing a person has to agree with in order to have a relationship with Christ."

We sat together and looked at the board for several minutes until we conceded we weren't going to come up with the missing element. I then erased the board and asked the class a different question: "What ideas would a guy need to agree with or what steps would a guy need to take in order to fall in love with a girl?" The class chuckled a bit, but I continued, going so far as to begin a list.

1. A guy would have to get to know her.

I stood back from the board and wondered out loud what the next step might be. "Any suggestions?" I asked the class. We thought about it for a second, and then one of the students spoke up and said, "It isn't exactly a scientific process."

The Gospel: A Relational Dynamic

Perhaps the reason Scripture includes so much poetry in and outside the narrative, so many parables and stories, so many visions and emotional letters, is because it is attempting to describe a *relational* break man tragically experienced with God and a disturbed *relational* history man has had since then and, furthermore, a *relational* dynamic man must embrace in order to have *relational* intimacy with God once again, thus healing himself of all the crap he gets into while looking for a *relationship* that makes him feel whole. Maybe the gospel of Jesus, in other words, is all about our relationship with Jesus rather than about ideas. And perhaps our lists and formulas and bullet points are nice in the sense that they help us memorize different truths, but harmful in the sense that they blind us to the necessary relationship that must begin between ourselves and God for us to become His followers. And worse, perhaps our formulas and bullet points and steps steal the sincerity with which we might engage God.

Becoming a Christian might look more like falling in love than baking cookies. Now don't get me wrong. I am not saying that in order for a person to know Jesus they must get a kind of crush on Him. But what I am suggesting is that, not unlike any other relationship, a person might need to understand that Jesus is alive, that He exists, that He is God, that He is in authority, that we need to submit to Him, that He has the power to save, and so on and so on, all of which *are* ideas, but ideas entangled in a kind of relational dynamic. This seems more logical to me because if God made us, wants to know us, then this would require a more mysterious interaction than what would be required by following a kind of recipe.

I realize it all sounds terribly sentimental, but imagine the other ideas popular today that we sometimes hold up as credible. We believe a person will gain access to heaven because he is knowledgeable about theology, because he can win at a game of religious trivia. And we may believe a person will find heaven because she is very spiritual and lights incense and candles and takes bubble baths and reads books that speak of centering her inner self; and some of us believe a person is a Christian because he believes five ideas that

Jesus communicated here and there in Scripture, though never completely at one time and in one place; and some people believe they are Christians because they do good things and associate themselves with some kind of Christian morality; and some people believe they are Christians because they are Americans. If any of these models are true, people who read the Bible before we systematically broke it down, and, for that matter, people who believed in Jesus before the printing press or before the birth of Western civilization, are at an extreme disadvantage. It makes you wonder if we have fashioned a gospel around our culture and technology and social economy rather than around the person of Christ.

It doesn't make a great deal of sense that a person who went to Bible college should have a better shot at heaven than a person who didn't, and it doesn't make a lot of sense either that somebody sentimental and spiritual has greater access. I think it is more safe and more beautiful and more true to believe that when a person dies he will go and be with God because, on earth, he had come to know Him, that he had a relational encounter with God not unlike meeting a friend or a lover or having a father or taking a bride, and that in order to engage God he gave up everything, repented and changed his life, as this sort of extreme sacrifice is what is required if true love is to grow. We would expect nothing less in a marriage; why should we accept anything less in becoming unified with Christ?

In fact, I have to tell you, I believe the Bible is screaming this idea and is completely silent on any other, including our formulas and bullet points. It seems, rather, that Christ's parables, Christ's words about eating His flesh and drinking His blood, were designed to bypass the memorization of ideas and cause us to wrestle with a certain need to cling to Him. In other words, a poetic presentation of the gospel of Jesus is more accurate than a set of steps.

Biblically, you are hard-pressed to find theological ideas divorced from their relational context. There are, essentially, three dominant metaphors describing our relationship with God: sheep to a shepherd, child to a father, and bride to a bridegroom. The idea of Christ's disciples being His mother and father and brothers and sisters is also presented. In fact, few places in Scripture speak to the Christian conversion experience through any method other than relational metaphor.

Contrasting this idea, I recently heard a man, while explaining how a person could *convert* to Christianity, say the experience was not unlike deciding to sit in a chair. He said that while *a person can have faith that a chair will hold him, it is not until he sits in the chair that he has acted on his faith.*

I wondered as I heard this if the chair was a kind of a symbol for Jesus, and how irritated Jesus might be if a lot of people kept trying to sit on Him.

And then I wondered at how Jesus could say He was a Shepherd and we were sheep, and that the Father in heaven was our Father and we were His children, and that He Himself was a Bridegroom and we were His bride, and that He was a King and we were His subjects, and yet we somehow missed His meaning and thought becoming a Christian was like sitting in a chair.

The Gospel of Ideas

So removed is our understanding of the gospel as a relational invitation that recently, while teaching another class of Bible college students, I presented a form of the gospel but left out a key element, to see if they would notice. I told them in advance that I was going to leave out a critical element of the gospel, and I asked them to listen carefully to figure out the missing piece.

I told them man was sinful, and this was obvious when we looked at the culture we lived in. I pointed out specific examples of depravity including homosexuality, abortion, drug use, song lyrics on the radio, newspaper headlines, and so on. Then I told the class that man must repent, and showed them Scriptures that spoke firmly of this idea. I used the true-life example I heard from a preacher about a man in Missouri who, warning people of a bridge that had collapsed, shot a flare gun directly at oncoming cars so they would stop before they drove over the bridge to their deaths. I said I was like that man, shooting flares at cars, and they could be mad at me and frustrated, but I was saving their lives, because the wages of sin is death, and they had to repent in order to see heaven. I then pointed to Scripture about the wages of sin being death, and talked at length about how sin separates us from God.

Then I spoke of the beauty of morality, and told a story of a friend who chose not to cheat on his wife and so now enjoys the fruits of his marriage, committed in love to his wife, grateful that he never betrayed the purity and beauty of their relationship. I talked about heaven and how great it will be to walk on streets of gold and how there will probably be millions of miles of mountains and rivers and how great it will be to fish those rivers and sit with our friends around a fire beneath a mountain peak that reaches up into stars so thick we could barely imagine the beauty of the expanse. I gave the class statistics regarding teen pregnancy and sexually transmitted diseases, going into detail about what it is they would be saved from if they would only repent, and how their lives could be God-honoring and God-centered and this would give them a sense of purity and a feeling of fulfillment on earth, and that God would provide for them in relationships and in finances and in comfort.

When I was done, I rested my case and asked the class if they could tell me what it was I had left out of this gospel presentation. I waited as a class of Bible college students—who that year had read several textbooks about Christian theology, who had read the majority of the Bible, all of whom had taken an evangelism class only weeks before in which they went door-to-door to hundreds of homes and shared their faith using pamphlets that explained the gospel, who had grown up in Christian homes attending strong evangelical churches, who had taken both New Testament Introduction and Old Testament Introduction—sat there for several minutes in uncomfortable silence.

None of the forty-five students in the class realized I had presented a gospel without once mentioning the name of Jesus.

The story bears repeating: I presented a gospel to Christian Bible college students and left out Jesus. Nobody noticed, even when I said I was going to neglect something very important, even when I asked them to think very hard about what it was I had left out, even when I stood there for several minutes in silence.

To a culture that believes they "go to heaven" based on whether or not they are morally pure, or whether they understand some theological ideas, or they are very spiritual, Jesus is completely unnecessary. At best, He is an afterthought, a technicality by which we become morally pure, or a subject of which we know, or a founding father of our woo-woo spirituality.

I assure you, these students loved Jesus very much, and they were terrific kids whom I loved being with, it's just that when they thought of the gospel, they thought of the message in terms of a series of thoughts or principles, not mysterious relational dynamics. The least important of the ideas, to this class, was knowing Jesus; the least important of the ideas was the one that is relational. The gospel of Jesus, then, mistakenly assumed by this class, is something different from Jesus Himself. The two are mutually exclusive in this way.

This, of course, is a lie birthed out of a method of communication the Bible never uses.

The Golden Cow

When the church began to doubt its own integrity after the Darwinian attack on Genesis 1 and 2, we began to answer science, not by appealing to something greater, the realm of beauty and art and spirituality, but by attempting to translate spiritual realities through scientific equations, thus justifying ourselves to culture, as if culture had some kind of authority to redeem us in the first place. Terms such as "absolute truth" and "inherency" (a term used only to describe Scripture in the last one hundred years or so) became a battle cry, even though the laws of absolute truth must, by their nature, exclude ideas such as *Jesus is the Word, He is both God and Man, the Trinity is both three and One,* we are *united with Him in His death,* because these are mysterious ideas, not scientific ideas.

In fact, much of biblical truth must go out the window when you approach it through the scientific method. God does not live within the philosophical science He made, any more than He is bound by the natural realities of gravity. There is moral law, to be sure, but moral law is not our path to heaven; our duty involves knowing and being known by Christ. Positive morality, then, the stuff of natural law, is but an offering, a sweet-tasting fruit in the mouth of God. It is obedience and an imitation of our pure and holy Maker; and immorality—the act of ignoring the conscience and the precepts of goodness—is a dagger in God's heart.

Because we have approached faith through the lens of science, the rich legacy of art that once flowed out of the Christian community has dried up. The poetry of Scripture, especially in the case of Moses, began to be interpreted literally and mathematically, and whole books such as the Song of Songs were completely and totally ignored. They weren't scientific. You couldn't break them down into bullet points. Morality became a code, rather than a manifestation of a love for Christ, the way a woman is faithful to her husband, the way a man is faithful to his wife. These relational ideas were replaced with wrong and right, good and bad, with only hinted suggestions as to where wrong and right and good and bad actually came from. Old Testament stories became formulas for personal growth rather than stories to help us understand the character and nature of the God with whom we interact.

In a culture that worships science, relational propositions will always be left out of arguments attempting to surface truth. We believe, quite simply, that unless we can chart something, it doesn't exist. And you can't chart relationships. Furthermore, in our attempts to make relational propositions look like chartable realities, all beauty and mystery is lost. And so when times get hard, when reality knocks us on our butts, mathematical propositions are unable to comfort our failing hearts. How many people have walked away from faith because their systematic theology proved unable to answer the deep longings and questions of the soul? What we need here, truly, is faith in a Being, not a list of ideas.

And one should not think our current method of interpreting Scripture has an ancient legacy. The modern view of Scripture originated in an age of industrial revolution when corporations were becoming more important than family (the husband, for the first time, left the home and joined Corporate America, building cars instead of families), and productivity was more important than relationships. *How can God help me get what I want?* was the idea, not *Who is God, and how can I know Him?*

Imagine a pamphlet explaining the gospel of Jesus that said something like this:

> You are the bride to the Bridegroom, and the Bridegroom is Jesus Christ. You must eat of His flesh and drink of His blood to know Him, and your union with Him will make you one, and your oneness with Him will allow you to be identified with Him, His purity allowing God to interact with you, and because of this you will be with Him in eternity, sitting at His side and enjoying His companionship, which will be more fulfilling than an earthly husband or an earthly bride. All you must do to engage God is be willing to leave everything behind, be willing to walk away from your identity, and embrace joyfully the trials and tribulations, the torture and perhaps martyrdom that will come upon you for being a child of God in a broken world working out its own redemption in empty pursuits.

Though it sounds absurd, this is a much more accurate summation of the gospel of Jesus than the bullet points we like to consider when we think about Christ's message to humanity.

In the third chapter of John, some Pharisees come out to talk with John the Baptist because Jesus has been baptizing people in a nearby river, thus threatening their position in the community as the people who do the baptizing. The Pharisees are furious and hoping to get John to join them in their hostility toward Jesus.

John answers them by saying, essentially, "Look, I told you I wasn't the Messiah, but rather the one who comes before Him to get everything ready. The One who gets the bride is the Bridegroom, by definition; but I am just His friend. I am like the best man in the wedding. And I am very happy about this. How could I be jealous when I know that the wedding is finished and the marriage is off to a great start?"

And Matthew in his gospel captures a conversation between Jesus and a group who were the disciples of John the Baptist. The disciples of John the Baptist are frustrated because they are fasting and Jesus' disciples are eating. They say to Him, "Why do we and the Pharisees fast, but your disciples do not fast?" And Jesus says to them, "The attendants of the Bridegroom cannot mourn as long as the Bridegroom is with them, can they? But the days will come when the Bridegroom is taken away from them, and then they will fast" (see Matthew 9:14–15).

In this way, Jesus takes the spiritual disciplines, the steps and actions religious folks had come to understand as a sort of spiritual checklist, and explains them as being deeply connected to a relational exchange. We fast because we mourn the absence of Christ.

At Imago Dei, the church I attend here in Portland, the congregation is invited to the front of the church after each service to dip bread into wine, partaking in one of the two sacraments given to those of us who are following Christ. And yet often, as I wait in line, go to the table, take the bread, and dip it into the cup of wine, I forget that the bread and wine I eat and drink are of absolutely no spiritual significance at all, that they have no more power than the breakfast I ate that morning, that what Jesus wanted was for us to eat the bread and drink the wine as a way of *remembering Him*, the bread representing His flesh, that He was a Man who, come from heaven, walked the earth with us and felt our pains, wept at our transgressions and humbly beckoned us to follow Him; and the wine is a symbol of the fact that He was killed, that His body was nailed to a cross, and that He entered into death, dying to absolve our need to die, our need to experience the ramifications of falling away and apart from God.

I confess that at times I have thought of Communion as a religious pill a person takes in order to check it off his list, and that the pill is best taken under the sedation of heavy mood music, or in silence.

How odd would it seem to have been one of the members of the early church, shepherded by Paul or Peter, and to come forward a thousand years to see people standing in line or sitting quietly in a large building that looked like a schoolroom or movie theater to take Communion. How different it would seem from the way they did it, sitting around somebody's living room table, grabbing a hunk of bread and holding their own glass of wine, exchanging stories about Christ, perhaps laughing, perhaps crying, consoling each other, telling one another that the Person who had exploded into their hearts was indeed the Son of God, their Bridegroom, come to tell them who they were, come to mend the broken relationship, come to marry them in a spiritual union more beautiful, more intimate than anything they could know on earth.

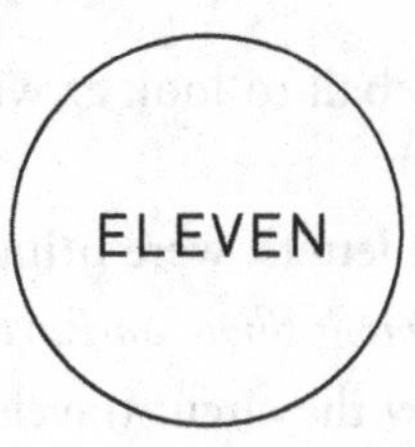

A Circus of Redemption

Why a Three-Legged Man Is Better Than a Bearded Woman

There's been a load of compromisin'
On the road to my horizon
But I'm gonna be where the lights are shinin' on me:
Like a rhinestone cowboy
Riding out on a horse in a star-spangled rodeo
Like a rhinestone cowboy
Getting cards and letters from people I don't even know
And offers comin' over the phone.

—Glen Campbell, "Rhinestone Cowboy"

Several months ago I was at a train station in Oakland in the middle of the night, sitting in the cold because my train to Portland was late. And while waiting, another train pulled into the station, a streamlined train, something you would see in the fifties crossing America on the news; the sort of long, shiny bullet rig kids would stop playing baseball to look at with their jaws open.

And on the side of this train, in great red letters, were printed the words *Barnum and Bailey Circus, The Greatest Show on Earth.*

Before Oakland, if you had asked me how the circus travels, I might have told you they had four or five trucks to haul animals around, and the people who work in the circus traveled by plane, or maybe they went around on buses. I don't know how I would have broken it down, if you had asked me, but I certainly wouldn't have told you they go around in a bullet train from the fifties. It got me wondering whether the circus travels by train because it is the most efficient way to travel, or whether they travel by train to feel romantic. But if you ask me, you don't need an old train to feel romantic about the circus. The circus is pretty romantic as it is. The thing that gets me feeling romantic, or sentimental, about a circus is the elephants.

When I was a kid my mother would take my sister and me to the circus. I had a timid nature, and our cheap seats were often very high in the arena, so the first twenty minutes of the circus I would spend gripping the armrests of my chair, always feeling that the floor was tipping forward into the great chasm of the arena, always imagining myself tumbling over the people in front of me, and in front of them, and over a railing to my death. I imagined things like this all the time when I was a kid.

When the circus came through Houston they brought a man who rode a motorcycle inside a large suspended cage shaped like a globe. He would kick-start his motorcycle, rev the two-stroke to excite the crowd, then slowly release the clutch to get the thing going around in a small circle at the bottom of the globe. He would circle the orb slowly at first, then faster, all the while riding higher into the sphere until, in dramatic fashion and to the tune of suspenseful music, he would ride with his body and bike entirely vertical. All this made me very nervous, and at this point in the show I would grip the armrests ever tighter and, seconds later, when the man on the motorcycle started riding in loops so his body was completely upside down at the top of each rotation, I felt as though the floor had vaporized and I was free-falling. I have always been like this, living vicariously through the risks of other people. My body can hardly hold the stress. You don't ever want to go to a movie with a guy like me because I am on the edge of my seat squirming, leaning in next to you saying things like *Can you believe this guy?*

Living vicariously through people is not a good thing when you are at a circus. As soon as the guy on the motorcycle finished, they brought out another guy, who walked across a piece of rope at the very top of the arena. The guy didn't even have a net, if you can believe it. My legs were jelly because he shook and stammered, the rope beneath him jerking suddenly left, then right, and when he had to lean over to keep his balance I nearly threw up on my sister, who, the entire time, was giving me these tired looks and saying things like, "Would you calm down? For heaven's sake, he does this for a living."

The only thing I really liked about the circus was the elephants. That is what I was telling you about. If you are going to live vicariously through something at a circus, and you don't want to throw up about it, your best bet is to live vicariously through an elephant. Here's what they do: They walk in a line holding each other's tails, they go into the middle ring and stand there for a little while, then they put a foot on a big stool and then they sit down like a dog waiting for a stick. The whole thing takes about twenty minutes, and it is consoling.

As a point of reference, ever since childhood, elephants have affected me as a calming mechanism. When I see them at the zoo, my heart slows, my nerves loosen, my skin cools, and my muscles relax.

I say this only because, sitting in the train station in Oakland, thinking back on the circus in Houston, I heard an elephant. They have a distinct sound, like a drunk man playing a tuba.

My muscles went to jelly and I turned my head slowly as the sound was coming from down the platform, from the darkness at the bend of the train, and like a man in a trance I stood to my relaxed legs and stepped one fluffy foot then another till the platform stopped. I stood there looking into the black when another of them called. I stepped off the platform onto the rocks, following the elephant's tuba around a bend till I could see them, in tall, prison-like cages set atop platform cars on the train. The holes in the cages were sparse, so I could see only the eye of one and the trunk of another, and their enormous feet, their umbrella-stand feet with toenails as big as my head and legs as round as redwoods.

There was, in my heart, a kind of calm euphoria. I felt as though I had been raised by these elephants years ago in the deep jungles of Africa, and we were being reunited in Oakland. Of course, none of this was true, but the thought of it was making the moment daydreamy.

Less daydreamy were a couple of people who had come out of a passenger car to smoke cigarettes. There was one man and one woman, one car before the cages, and the man was wearing jeans and the woman looked as though she had just put on her clothes, her T-shirt and pajama pants and flip-flop shoes. Her disheveled hair and red cheeks came to lips on her cigarette.

"May I get closer to the elephants?" I asked her, ignoring, as it were, her obvious concern for her appearance.

"What's that, darlin'?" The woman pretended not to have

heard me, tilting her head up and pursing her lips to blow smoke into the air.

"May I look at the elephants?" I asked again.

The man turned and looked at me in distrust, seeming more concerned about my interference with him and the woman than with him and the elephants.

"Sure, darlin'. Look all you want," the woman spoke.

I walked to the edge of a cage and peered in through one of the holes. Their smell was enormous. Their eyes were as large as softballs, set deep into caves of moist gray. Their ears hung down like curtains, torn and scarred, showing pink in birthmarks or age. They moved slowly, purposefully, and embodied the kind of dignity that happens with weight and size.

I won't tell you how I realized at that moment that elephants shouldn't be in cages. I won't tell you how I think they should all live in Africa, or on the streets of Oakland going where they want, so cars have to stop and wait for them to pass, and people have to take off their hats when they walk by, and how everybody should refer to elephants as sir or ma'am, saying, *Nice day for a walk, isn't it, ma'am?* so the elephants could blow their tubas in agreement.

"I don't know why he even keeps Marcus around," the man said, and I thought he was talking to me.

"Pardon me?" I said to him.

"I wasn't talking to you," the man said matter-of-factly, holding his cigarette away from his body, then thumping it with his thumb, then turning again to the woman.

"Pay no attention to him, darlin'. He's just a grumpy old man," the woman told me, excusing me for interrupting their conversation.

"That's okay," I told her, feeling half my age, half my maturity, standing in the darkness looking at elephants.

"He don't make any money for the company," the man continued with the woman. "Nobody wants to see a man shoot flaming arrows at a target."

"Well, he does throw knives. Monica told me the thing isn't a trick, either, that she actually stands there and closes her eyes. One of them cut her on the ear."

"That thing ain't no trick?" the man asked. *That thing isn't a trick?* I wondered, fascinated, as it were, at the conversations that take place in circus life. I kept looking at the elephants, but I was secretly paying attention to the conversation between the man and the woman, pretending, in my head, that I was a person who worked for a circus, too, and we were concerned about job security, about whether or not they were going to get rid of me and my elephants.

"Monica said it was real," the woman continued. "Real knives, really flying at her."

"Don't make any difference at all," the man said loudly. "You can't see how close a knife is to a woman's ear when you're up in the cheap seats."

And what the man was saying was true, because I had been in the cheap seats.

"If they're going to lay off anybody, they're going to lay him off," the man said with relief in his voice.

"They aren't going to cut him, Billy. He knows Roger, he and Roger go way back, and he is on for good. And they aren't going to cut the Lipton family, either. The Lipton family has been doing that stupid trapeze thing for fifty years; they've got some sort of eternal contract. It's you and me; that's the ones who are going to get cut." And the woman said this in a somber tone, with worry in her voice.

"And replace us with what?" the man said. "Media? All that

television and music screaming up the place. That ain't real entertainment. That ain't real circus. You know it ain't." The man threw his cigarette on the ground and stared into the darkness toward the platform. "The animals are all staying." The man started talking again. "I should have taken that job with Bernie when she asked me. I'd rather feed a bunch of horses all the time than be back on the street."

"You aren't going to be back on the street," she said comfortingly.

"Like you know that." The man stood there for a second, then turned and looked at me looking at the two of them.

"Elephants ain't that interesting?" he questioned, meaning I was being nosy. And he watched me as I walked away from the elephants, sort of kicking rocks and acting like their conversation wasn't interesting.

By the time I got back to the platform the train was moving, and the woman was standing in the doorway of a passenger car when it passed, still smoking a cigarette, and she looked at me and I looked at her and she looked sad, didn't even bother to smile, just looked right through me with a kind of worry in her eyes. I waved at her and she nodded.

I sat down on the bench on the platform and wondered what it was the man and woman did for the circus. I wondered whether or not they were clowns or something, like them and twenty friends get in a little car, drive to the center ring, and get out one at a time. Or maybe they dance around in sexy outfits and he lifts her up and onto a hula hoop and balances her on his nose. I'll bet they weren't any of those things, though. I'll bet they were just a couple of people on a crew who put up a tent or put together that metal globe the guy with the motorcycle uses. And I'll bet the guy with the motorcycle gets to go everywhere on a plane or in an RV, and these two have to go around in a bullet train, wondering how long they will have their jobs.

—

It can't be easy doing that sort of thing. Working in a circus. I read a book a while back about women with beards and men who could swallow swords. In this book there were people who ate fire and nails, a man with hands like crab pincers, and a lady with tattoos across her entire body: Up from her stomach was a great flame that turned to smoke and ashes of burning pages of poetry that rose across her breasts and up her shoulders to the chimney plume of her neck.

All these people were living in America between the two wars, traveling in a sideshow. They sat on stages in small theaters, and for a quarter you could go in and look at them. There was a caller who stood outside on a platform and hyped their unique, odd, and eerie features to fathers and sons, mothers behind them gasping at the descriptions, and daughters downright frightened. And the more spooked the women were made to feel, the more willing the men were to pay the admission and prove how brave they were.

There was a movement in those days to end the shows; protesters claimed they exploited the deformed. But the acts in the show were paid handsomely and so did battle in the papers with their supposed allies, claiming that if not for the show itself, they were largely unemployable. "Who wants to hire a woman with a beard?" one of the performers explained passionately. "We understand each other," another went on to say. "We have a community, a group of people who, because of their own deformities, accept the deformity in others. We are the lucky ones, because we understand that people are only people, that the thing you think makes you better than us is an illusion."

And yet, as the book continues, the author paints a clear hierarchy within the community. There was, among the ten or so characters, a man with three legs. He had been hired out of Chicago, a late entry to the company. After five or six shows, the caller, who also employed the team of odd talent, shifted the three-legged man to the final appearance in the show. Though the man could walk normally, for the act he dressed in sloppy large clothes and worked his hair into a frenzy. He stammered onto stage in a daze and walked the corners of the platform, swinging his body left and right, acting at once angered and terrified at the crowd. Each time he turned his body, his third leg swung out and startled the women and children. The act was so rousing that during a performance in New York, the three-legged performer got too close to the audience and was attacked by a man attempting to protect his wife from an accidental touch.

Far from being offended by the assault or feeling victimized, the three-legged man was thrilled. When the attack made the papers, the caller no longer had to stir the crowd. There was a line for a quarter mile. And a press statement detailing the incident in New York was released by the show in every city visited that year. The three-legged man's salary was at once doubled, which enraged the other talent, nearly destroying the community. No longer was a man with three legs on even par with a bearded woman. A hierarchy had been created: three legs beating two; female facial hair, apparently, beating crab hands; and all this was decided by the response of the crowd.

"Not everybody is lucky enough to get born with three legs," the bearded woman said. "It's not like he did anything to deserve that kind of blessing."

What odd sort of hierarchy is created when a group tunnels beneath the surface of normal community, I thought to myself while reading the book.

For months after reading the book I contemplated the community, how, as a normal person, I would gain no favor from an audience and have no commodity in the small outfit of misfits. They would probably have felt sorry for me, in fact, watching me walk onstage night after night so the audience could shrug their shoulders as I sat on an empty stage and typed words into a computer. The audience would boo me after a while because what I do is so boring, and I would probably be very upset about it and feel dejected, until finally the guy who ran the show would call me into a trailer and explain, very kindly, that I wasn't meant for the sideshow, that I just wasn't very entertaining. And I would probably be jealous of the man with three legs, too, because in that tiny traveling population, he was a rock star, a mayor of sorts.

And here is an odd idea: Were any of us to close ourselves off so our social nourishment came exclusively from these performers, if any of us were to travel with them, it is inevitable that we would become jealous of the more freakish characters. It seems that when a group of people come together, they will develop a kind of hierarchy of importance, and the determining factors of a person's value are not only unfair but arbitrary. Where you and I might become upset at God over having too great a nose or too hairy a back, these few feel dejection about the *normality* of their bodies.

The reason I took the trip to Oakland in the first place was to speak at a church across the bay. I realized, sitting there at the train station, thinking about the circus performers, that I was just like them. What I mean is, while I spoke at the church I wondered how the audience was perceiving what I was saying, and I wondered whether any of them were being moved, and I wondered if I was funny enough or smart enough to engage a thousand people. And I feel the same way about my books and about my life in general. The circus, and I am talking about life now, really sucks. It feels like we all have these little acts, these stupid things we do that we all hang our hats on. The Fall has made monkeys of us, for crying out loud. Some of us are athletes and others of us are physicists, and some of us are good-looking and some of us are rich, and we all are running around, in a way, trying to get a bunch of people to clap for us, trying to get a bunch of people to say we are normal, we are healthy, we are good. And there is nothing wrong with being beautiful or being athletic or being smart, but those are some of the pleasures of life, not life's redemption.

Do you know what Paul said about the stuff he wrote and taught? He said he didn't write with big and fancy words to try to impress people; rather, he just told the truth, God's truth, and let that be what it was, powerful and honest, making sense of life.

The thing about being a monkey is that it affects all our relationships. One writer has said that what we commonly think of as love is really the desire to be loved. I know that is true for me, and it has been true for years, that often when I want somebody to like me, I am really wanting them to say that I am redeemed, that I am not a loser, that I can stay in the boat, stay in the circus, that my act redeems me.

In this sense, as harsh as some of Jesus' words are, they are also beautiful and comforting. No more worrying about what an audience thinks, no more trying to elbow our way to the top. We have Him instead, a God who redeems our identity *for* us, giving us His righteousness.

I read this painful passage in Eugene Peterson's translation of the book of Galatians the other day that sums up life in the lifeboat, life in the circus:

> It is obvious what kind of life develops out of trying to get your own way all the time: repetitive, loveless, cheap sex; a stinking accumulation of mental and emotional garbage; frenzied and joyless grabs for happiness; trinket gods; magic-show religion; paranoid loneliness; cutthroat competition; all-consuming-yet-never-satisfied wants; a brutal temper; an impotence to love or be loved; divided homes and divided lives; small-minded and lopsided pursuits; the vicious habit of depersonalizing everyone into a rival; uncontrolled and uncontrollable addictions; ugly parodies of community. I could go on.
>
> (Galatians 5:19–21 THE MESSAGE)

I kept thinking about all this and I wanted it all to end. I didn't want to be a part of it anymore. Paul kept writing in his books about how people shouldn't want to be circumcised anymore, about how people shouldn't think they were better than other people, about how folks should submit to one another in love, thinking of each other as more important than themselves, and I know now, and I realized back in Oakland, that this kind of life could take place only within a relationship with God, the One who takes care of our needs, the One who really has the power to tell us who we are, if we would only trust in Him.

Imagine how much a man's life would be changed if he trusted that he was loved by God? He could interact with the poor and not show partiality, he could love his wife easily and not expect her to redeem him, he would be slow to anger because redemption was no longer at stake, he could be wise and giving with his money because money no longer represented points, he could give up on formulaic religion, knowing that checking stuff off a spiritual to-do list was a worthless pursuit, he would have confidence and the ability to laugh at himself, and he could love people without expecting anything in return. It would be quite beautiful, really.

Do you know what King David did one time when he was worshiping God? He took off all his clothes and danced around in the street. Everybody was watching him and he didn't care. His poor wife was completely embarrassed, but David didn't worry, he didn't care what anybody thought about him; he just took off his clothes before God and danced.

Don't get me wrong, I have no intention of taking off my clothes on Sunday morning at church. I bring this up only to say there is a certain freedom in getting our feelings of redemption from God and not other people. This is what we have always wanted, isn't it? And it isn't the American dream at all, it is the human dream, the deepest desire of our hearts.

I would imagine, then, that the repentance we are called to is about choosing one audience over another. Jesus says many times in the gospel that He knows the heart of man, and the heart of man does not have the power to give glory. I think Jesus is saying, *Look, you guys are running around like monkeys trying to get people to clap, but people are fallen, they are separated from God, so they have no idea what is good or bad, worthy to be judged or set free, beautiful or ugly to begin with. Why not get your glory from God? Why not accept your feelings of redemption because of His pleasure in you, not the fickle and empty favor of man? And only then will you know who you are, and only then will you have true, uninhibited relationships with others.*

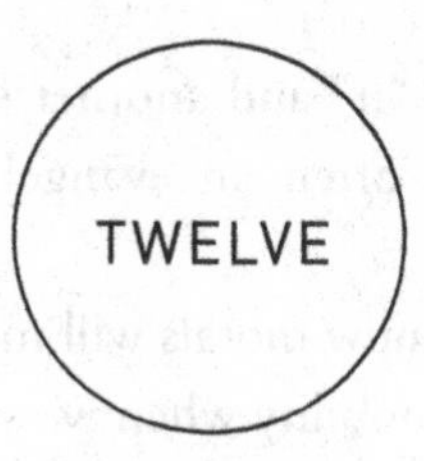

Morality

Why I Am Better Than You

A great concern for those who defend a propositional gospel over a relational gospel is morality. Some feel that if we do not emphasize morality, people will have too much fun and refuse to play by the rules the rest of us who know God have to play by. But I don't think this is true. I've heard it said that Mormonism is the fastest-growing religion and my guess is, the fast growth is because it offers a strict morality, a system of rights and wrongs that people can live by as well as accountability, so they don't cheat on their spouses or kick their dogs. All of us subscribe to some kind of morality, born mostly of a conscience rather than a book. And the Bible is not structured as a moral code. It does not have all the answers on right and wrong. It has some, enough to guide a man's conscience, but a book containing a complete moral code would require all pages in all books.

Somehow, and for some reason, each of us subscribes to a kind of morality, and though for some this code is not defined, it is understood and adhered to. Grievances, then, are disagreements in the moral code, not one side holding to "it" and another side disregarding "it," which, unfortunately, is often an evangelical position.

The truth is, we all want morality. We know morals will make us better people, and we even feel a kind of nobility when we subscribe to and defend a code. I watched a documentary recently about young African-American men in urban New York City who are turning in droves to Islam because of its moral guidance. Each of the young men was looking for a father figure, for a mentor who would provide for him boundaries, understanding intrinsically that life has rules and parameters and to succeed in the soul, one must learn these parameters. Don't get me wrong, I don't believe Muhammad was a true prophet, but I enjoyed watching this documentary because it reminded me that I, too, have parameters and rules with which to navigate my existence.

Lately, however, I have been thinking of morality in less conceptual terms, less as a system of rules and regulations and more as a concept very beautiful and alive. Please do not think I am blurring the lines between right and wrong; rather, I am wanting to bring these lines to life to reveal a guide and a judge. The reason I have been feeling this way is not because morality gives us boundaries or because it helps us live clean lives, though morality does these things, but rather because, in some mysterious way, morality pleases God.

One of the great problems with morality for me in the past was that it didn't seem to be connected to anything. I no longer believe morality will redeem me. What I mean by this is that, often, when I had lustful thoughts, greedy thoughts, and envious thoughts, or for that matter performed lustful actions, actions that stemmed from greed or envy, I felt that I would go to hell for doing them, for thinking these things.

Growing up in a small conservative church in the South, you hear more about morality than you do about Christ. If you were immoral, if you danced, drank, or cussed, you were made to feel that God no longer liked you. And if you were moral, you were made to feel not one with Christ, but right and good and better than other people. These things were not stated directly, but the environment left me with this impression. Christian spirituality, then, hinged on whether or not a person behaved.

I don't mean any of this to suggest I don't want to behave, or that I want to go on sinning and say that it is okay with God. There is no part of me that believes anything like this can be defended scripturally. A god who says everybody can do as they please would be a bad god, a bad father, giving license for anarchy. Love creates rules, and forgives when they are broken. People would hurt themselves if they did anything they wanted. People do hurt themselves and others all the time by neglecting laws and rules.

What I really wanted, though, was a *reason* for morals, a reason stronger than somebody's simple suggestion that right was right and wrong was wrong.

When David wrote his Twenty-third Psalm he indicated God led him in the paths of righteousness for *His* name's sake. This struck me, recently, when I was reading through the Psalms. I had always thought morality was something God created exclusively to keep mankind out of the ditches, and to a large degree I suppose this is true, but David's concept of morality was quite new to me and I wondered exactly what he meant by the phrase "for His name's sake."

Peter would argue in the book of Acts that when David talked about the Lord, he was talking about Jesus, acting as a kind of prophet. And in this light, the Twenty-third Psalm becomes quite beautiful. The Valley of the Shadow of Death, I came to learn while studying the passage, is an actual valley outside Jerusalem. It is treacherous terrain, and shepherds once herded sheep through this valley to move them to green pastures and fresh water. There were crags in the rocks, ditches, and thornbushes that sheep, simple as they are, would fall into, so shepherds had to use their staffs, those big sticks with the rounded hooks on the end, to reach into the crags and ditches to rescue the sheep. And the shepherd also had a rod he would use to scare off wild animals, keeping the sheep safe in the passage. In the Twenty-third Psalm, David says, "Thy rod and thy staff they comfort me" (v. 4 KJV), and when I think of myself as a sheep, looking up at Jesus, who has a staff to rescue me and a rod to protect me, it makes me feel that this passage is quite endearing, that basically I am a simple sheep, having very little idea of what is right and wrong, and Jesus is going to pull me out of the ditches when I screw up, and protect me from spiritual enemies who, as we've already discussed, roam about like lions.

And then the words regarding Christ's leading us in the paths of righteousness come up, and I know David is talking about the safe ground through the Valley of the Shadow of Death, and how there is a right way, a way that is prudent, a way that doesn't have the crags and bushes; and this is the way of God's morality. That is, God's ethics, His conscience instilled in man and guided by Scripture, are the best ways to travel through a fallen world, through the Valley of the Shadow of Death, or what I have referred to as a lifeboat and a circus.

It made me wonder, then, if the idea of morality is just another ramification of the Fall. Paul even says that the law was given to the Jews to show them they couldn't follow the law, to reveal to them the depravity of human nature, to show them the cancer that lived inside them so they would pay attention to the Doctor.

In my own life, I try to be moral, but I am no good at it. It becomes obvious, in my effort, that I have this cancer Paul alludes to, that I am in this fallen body with a fallen mind and a fallen nature. That said, I don't suppose we will have any kind of morality in heaven, any thought about right and wrong, once we are with God, once our minds and our bodies and our natures are replenished and healed in His light and His goodness. No, morality exists only because we are fallen, not unlike medicine exists because people get sick.

Morality, then, if you think about it, is the way we imitate God. It is the way we imitate the ways of heaven here on earth. Jesus says, after all, to know Him we must follow Him, we must cling to Him and imitate Him, and many places in Scripture the idea is presented that if we know Him, we will obey Him.

If you look for this relational concept of morality, you see it all through Scripture. Paul connects the idea of morality to Christ in the books of Ephesians and Romans, and the author of Hebrews directly connects morality to our relationship with God in several places in that text. John the Evangelist, in all three of his short books at the end of the Bible, keeps saying if we know God we will love our brother, and if we know God we will obey.

I was contacted by a magazine editor recently who asked if I would consider writing a few articles for his publication. The editor told me his magazine was unique in that both Christians and people who weren't Christians contributed, which allowed them to offer a wide variety of perspectives in an open-table format. I thought the magazine sounded terrific and asked him if he would send me a copy. A few days later the magazine arrived, and I took it to Powell's to sit and read in the coffee shop. I have to tell you, I didn't like what I read. The first article was a shabbily written diatribe against conventional concepts of morality. The writer said he was in a Christian rock band but didn't see himself as being any different from any other rock star, saying proudly that he frequently slept with his girlfriend, that he smoked pot and got drunk and applauded anybody who was willing to experiment. He went on to excuse his actions by claiming God's grace. I read the article a couple of times and realized, perhaps, what it was that David and Paul were speaking of when they connected morality to God's glory, and immorality to His personal pain.

Can you imagine being a bride in a wedding, walking down the aisle toward your bridegroom, and during the procession, checking out the other groomsmen, wondering when you could sneak off to sleep with one of them, not taking the marriage to your groom seriously? Paul became furious at the church in Corinth for allowing a man to sleep with his stepmother. It makes sense to think of this as Paul's protecting the beauty and grandeur of a union with Christ. In this way, immorality is terrible because it is cheating on the Creator, who loves us and offers Himself as a Bridegroom for the bride.

When I said I was looking for a *reason* for morality, this is what I meant. The motive is love, love of God and of my fellow man.

The hijacking of the concept of morality began, of course, when we reduced Scripture to formula and a love story to theology, and finally morality to rules. It is a very different thing to break a rule than it is to cheat on a lover. A person's mind can do all sorts of things his heart would never let him do. If we think of God's grace as a technicality, a theological precept, we can disobey without the slightest feeling of guilt, but if we think of God's grace as a relational invitation, an outreach of love, we are pretty much jerks for belittling the gesture.

In this way, it isn't only the moralist looking for a feeling of superiority who commits crimes against God, it is also those of us who react by doing what we want, claiming God's grace. Neither view of morality connects behavior to a relational exchange with Jesus. When I run a stop sign, for example, I am breaking a law against a system of rules, but if I cheat on my wife, I have broken a law against a person. The first is impersonal; the latter is intensely personal.

—

There are a great many other motives for morality, but in my mind they are less than noble. Morality for love's sake, for the sake of God and the sake of others, seems more beautiful to me than morality for morality's sake, morality to build a better nation here on earth, morality to protect our schools, morality as an identity for one of the parties in the culture war, one of the identities in the lifeboat.

I confess, when I was young my mind rebelled from the standard evangelical mantra about morality. My rebellion was reactionary, to be sure. I can't tell you how many times I have seen an evangelical leader on television talking about this *culture war*, about how we are being threatened by persons with an immoral agenda, and I can't tell you how many sermons I have heard in which immoral pop stars or athletes or politicians have been denounced because of their shortcomings. Rarely, however, have I heard any of these ideas connected with the dominant message of Christ, a message of grace and forgiveness and a call to repentance. Rather, the moral message I have heard is often a message of bitterness and anger because *our* morality, *our* culture, is being taken over by people who disregard *our* ethical standards. None of it was connected, relationally, to God at all.

In this way, it has felt like one group in the lifeboat, the moral group, is at odds with another group, the *immoral* group, and the fight is about dominance *in* a fallen system rather than rescue *from* a fallen system. And I wonder, *What good does it do to tell somebody to be moral so they can die fifty years later and, apparently, go to hell?*

It makes me wonder and even judge (confession) the motives of somebody who wages a culture war about morality without confessing their own immorality while pointing to the Christ who saved them, the Christ who wishes to rescue everybody.

Morality, in this way, can be a circus act, giving a person a feeling of superiority. And while morality is good, anything we do to get other people to clap, or anything that gives us a more prominent position in a sinking ship, runs the risk of replacing a humble nature pointed at Christ, who is our Redeemer. The biblical idea of morality is behavior associated with our relationship with Jesus, not bait for pride.

In fact, morality as a battle cry *against* a depraved culture is simply not a New Testament idea. Morality as a ramification of our spiritual union and relationship with Christ, however, is.

Paul said to the church at Rome that those who chose immorality would be given over to a depraved mind and their lives would be ruined, but in the next breath he said that because of his great love for lost people, he would be willing to go to hell and take God's wrath upon himself. And he said this even about the Jews who were persecuting him. In other words, the call to morality is delivered through a changed and forgiven heart, a heart regenerated and delivered by Christ, desiring that all people repent and come to know Him. There is nothing here we can use in the lifeboat at all. The agenda is all God's, not ours, and God's agenda is love.

I was thinking of Paul recently when I saw an evangelical

leader on CNN talking about gay marriage. The evangelical leader agreed with the apostle Paul about homosexuality being a sin, but when it came time to express the kind of love Paul expressed for the lost, the kind of love that says, *I would gladly take God's wrath upon myself and go to hell for your sake,* the evangelical leader sat in silence. Why? How can we say the rules Paul presented are true, but neglect the heart with which he communicated those rules?

My suspicion is the evangelical leader was able to do this because he had taken on the morality of God as an identity with which he was attempting to redeem himself to culture, and perhaps even to God. This is what the Pharisees did, and the same Satan tricks us with the same bait: justification through comparison. It's an ugly trick, but it continues to prove effective.

I was the guest on a radio show recently that was broadcast on a secular station, one of those conservative shows that paints Democrats as terrorists. The interviewer asked what I thought about the homosexuals who were trying to take over the country. I confess I was taken aback. I hadn't realized that homosexuals were trying to take over the country.

"Which homosexuals are trying to take over the country?" I asked.

"You know," the interviewer began, "the ones who want to take over Congress and the Senate."

I paused for a while. "Well," I said, "I've never met those guys and I don't know who they are. The only homosexuals I've met are very kind people, some of whom have been beat up and spit on and harassed and, in fact, feel threatened by the religious right." Think about it. If you watch CNN all day and see extreme

Muslims in the Middle East declaring war on America because they see us as immoral, and then you read the paper the next day to find the exact same words spoken by evangelical leaders against the culture here in America, you'd be pretty scared. I've never heard of a homosexual group trying to take over the world, or for that matter the House or the Senate, but I can point you to about fifty evangelical organizations who are trying to do exactly that. I don't know why. In my opinion, we should tell people about Jesus, not try to build some kind of temporary moral civilization here on earth. If you want that, move to Salt Lake City. "And what is the name of this homosexual group that is trying to take over America?" I asked the host, somewhat angry at his ignorant misuse of war rhetoric.

"Well, I hear about them all the time," he said, rather frustrated with me.

"If you hear about them all the time, what is the name of the organization?"

"Well, I don't know right now. But they are there."

"Can I list for you ten or so Christian organizations who are working to try to get more Christians in the House and the Senate?" I said to the host.

"Listen, I get your point," he said.

"But I don't think you do. Here is my position: As a Christian, I believe Jesus wants to reach out to people who are lost and, yes, immoral—immoral just like you and I are immoral; and declaring war against them and stirring up your listeners to the point of anger and giving them the feeling that their country, their families, and their lifestyles are being threatened is only hurting what Jesus is trying to do. This isn't rocket science. If you declare war on somebody, you have to either handcuff them or kill them. That's the only way to win. But if you want them to be forgiven by Christ, if you want them to live eternally in heaven with Jesus, then you have to love them. The choice is yours and my suspicion is you will be held responsible by God, a Judge who will know your motives. So go ahead and declare war in the name of a conservative agenda, but don't do it in the name of God. That's what militant Muslims are doing in the Middle East, and we don't want that here."

Amazingly, the host kept me on and allowed me to tell a story or two about interacting with supposed pagans in a compassionate exchange, and later even admitted that his idea that homosexuals were trying to take over the country had originated from an e-mail he had received, an e-mail he had long since thrown away but he thought perhaps had come from *some kind of homosexual organization.*

To be honest, I think most Christians, and this guy was definitely a Christian, want to love people and obey God but feel they *have* to wage a culture war. But this isn't the case at all. Remember, we are not elbowing for power in the lifeboat. God's kingdom isn't here on earth. And I believe you will find Jesus in the hearts of even the most militant Christians, moving them to love people, and it is only their egos, and the voice of Satan, that cause them to demean the lost. What we must do in these instances is listen to our consciences, and allow Scripture to instruct us about morality *and* methodology, not just morality.

Paul was deceived when he persecuted Christians, thinking he was doing it to serve God, but God went to him, blinded him, and corrected his thinking. After this, Paul loved the people he had previously hated; he began to take the message of forgiveness to Jews and to Gentiles, to male and to female, to pagans and prostitutes. At no point does he waste his time lobbying government for a moral agenda. Nobody in Scripture who knew and followed Jesus wasted their time with any of this; they built the church, they loved people.

Once Paul switched positions, many people tried to kill him

for talking about Jesus, but he never lifted a fist; he never declared war. In fact, in Athens, he was so appreciated by pagans who worshiped false idols, they invited him to speak about Jesus in an open forum. In America, this no longer happens. We are in the margins of society and so we have to have our own radio stations and television stations and bookstores. Our formulaic, propositional, lifeboat-territorial methodology has crippled the kingdom of God. We can learn a great deal from the apostles. Paul would go so far as to compliment the men of Athens, calling them "spiritual men" and quoting their poetry, then telling them the God he knew was better for them, larger, stronger, and more alive than any of the stone idols they bowed down to. And many of the people in the audience followed Him and had more and more questions. This would not have happened if Paul had labeled them as pagans and attacked them.

A moral message, a message of *us* versus *them*, overflowing in war rhetoric, never hindered the early message of grace, of repentance toward dead works and immorality in exchange for a love relationship with Christ. War rhetoric against people is not the methodology, not the sort of communication that came out of the mouth of Jesus or the mouths of any of His followers. In fact, even today, moralists who use war rhetoric will speak of right and wrong, and even some vague and angry god, but never Jesus. Listen closely, and I assure you, they will not talk about Jesus.

In my opinion, if you hate somebody because they are different from you, you'd best get on your knees and repent until you can say you love them, until you have gotten your soul right with Christ.

I can't say this clearly enough: If we are preaching morality without Christ, and using war rhetoric to communicate a battle mentality, we are fighting on Satan's side. This battle we are in is a battle against the principalities of darkness, not against people who are different from us. In war you shoot the enemy, not the hostage.

In this way, the chief difference between morality in a relational context to Jesus and morality in the context of the lifeboat is that one system works for people and the other against them.

It is obvious when reading Scripture that what you and I commonly think of as morality is thin in definition. Some Christians, when considering immorality in culture, consider two issues: abortion and gay marriage.

Moral ideas presented in the New Testament, and even from the mouth of Christ, however, involve loving our neighbors, being one in the bond of peace, loving our enemies, taking care of our own business before we judge somebody else, forgiving debts even as we have been forgiven, speaking in truth and love lest we sound like clanging cymbals (turn on Fox News to hear what clanging cymbals sound like), and protecting the beauty of sex and marriage.

Morality, then, becomes the bond, the glue that holds our families together, our communities together, and our churches together, and most important, builds intimacy with Christ. Morality, in the context of a relationship with Jesus, becomes the voice of love to a confused community, the voice of reason and calm in a loud argument, the voice of life in a world of walking dead, the voice of Christ in a sea of self-hatred.

The trick Satan has played on us involving his spin on morality has not gone unnoticed by those outside the church.

In his book *Lies and the Lying Liars Who Tell Them*, Al Franken included a provocative multipage comic strip about a man named Supply-Side Jesus. In the strip, Supply-Side Jesus walks through the streets of Jerusalem stating that people should start businesses so they can employ the poor and should purchase exotic and expensive clothes and jewelry so their money will trickle into the economy and, eventually, bring bread to the mouths of the starving.

In the comic, the disciples come to Supply-Side Jesus and say they want to feed the poor directly, but Supply-Side Jesus says no, that if you give money or food or water directly to the poor, you are only helping them in their laziness and increasing the welfare state. Eventually, Rome catches up with Supply-Side Jesus and, before an angry mob, Pontius Pilate asks the masses which man they want to crucify, Supply-Side Jesus or another man who, in the comic, stands beside Pilate humbly, a disheveled and shadowy figure. The crowd chants they want to free Supply-Side Jesus because they like his philosophies, and they want to crucify this other man, the shadowy figure standing next to Pilate. Pilate tells the crowd this other man is innocent, that he has done no wrong, but the crowd refuses to listen and instead chants, "Crucify him, crucify him." Pilate then lets Supply-Side Jesus go free, and orders the innocent man, whose name was Jesus of Nazareth, to be crucified.

I sat there reading the book at Horse Brass Pub in amazement. Here was Al Franken, a known liberal who often lambastes the conservative Christian right but who also, somehow, understands the difference between the Jesus the religious right worships and the Jesus presented in Scripture. One Jesus is understood through conservative economic theory, the other through the Gospels.

I recall watching a documentary detailing Muslim frustration, both domestic and Middle Eastern, with the perception that all Muslims subscribe to the sort of angry and dangerous extremism propagated by terrorist hijackers on September 11. "It was more than those planes that got hijacked," one Muslim woman commented. "It was the nation of Islam. In the eyes of the world, they took our faith and flew it into those buildings. The damage may never be repaired."

I wondered if the Christian faith in America had not been hijacked as well, hijacked by those same two issues: abortion and gay marriage. How did a spirituality such as Christianity, a spirituality that speaks of eternity, of a world without end, of forgiveness of sins and a mysterious union with the Godhead, come to be represented by a moralist agenda and a trickle-down economic theory? And more important, how did a man born of Eastern descent, a man who called Himself the Prince of Peace, a man whom the sacred writings describe eating with prostitutes and providing wine at weddings and healing the sick and ignoring any political plot, a man who wants us to turn the other cheek and give all our possessions if we are sued, become associated with—no, become the poster boy for—a Western moral and financial agenda communicated through the rhetoric of war and ignorant of the damage it is causing to a world living in poverty?

My only answer is that Satan is crafty indeed.

I realize there are people reading this who will automatically dismiss me as a theological liberal, but I do not believe a person can take two issues from Scripture, those being abortion and gay marriage, and adhere to them as sins, then neglect much of the rest and call himself a fundamentalist or even a conservative. The person who believes the sum of his morality involves gay marriage and abortion alone, and neglects health care and world trade and the environment and loving his neighbor and feeding the poor is, by definition, a theological liberal, because he takes what he wants from Scripture and ignores the rest. Make no mistake, there is a lifeboat motive in play, a *join a team and fight* feeling that is roaming around the world like a lion, searching to destroy men's souls.

—

The reason I bring this up is to plead with evangelicals to return to the sort of call Christ has given us, to obey Him and experience intimacy with Him through sharing our faith, loving our enemies, and serving and feeding the poor and hungry directly, and to stop showing off about how moral we are and how that makes us better than other people. I assure you, once we leave the fight over our country's future and enter the spiritual battle for the hearts and souls of the lost, the church will flourish, and the kingdom of God will grow. God is not in the business of brokering for power over a nation; He is in the business of loving the unloved and pulling sheep out of crags and bushes.

The greatest comfort I can feel in the middle of this is that Jesus did not lend Himself to war causes, to tax issues or political campaigns. For that matter, He did not lend Himself to raising money for education or stumping for affirmative action. It was as if He did not trust us to build a utopia. He kept it very simple, in fact. *Follow Me,* He said. *I have no opinion about what color the paint should be in this prison. Follow Me.*

Is Jesus angry? *Sometimes.* Does He speak of sin and morality? *Yes, quite frequently.* Does the contemporary evangelical model of sin and morality reflect the teachings of Christ? *As a flea is a part of a dog, but not to be confused with the dog itself.* Is Jesus frustrated with sinners? *Yes.* Is He frustrated with religious zealots who use His Father's name to build businesses or support agendas? *He is violently frustrated.* Is there a penalty to pay for rejecting Him? *Yes, apart from Christ we will die and are dying.* Does Jesus like liberals more than conservatives? *He will be nobody's flag.*

—

I suspect any lack of love or feelings of anger we have toward the culture around us are not feelings that come from God, but rather our souls arising again to cast rocks at women caught in adultery. We should not expect Christ to respond any differently to us than He did to the moralists of His day:

They dropped their stones and walked away, feeling ashamed that each of them had been proved a sinner, too. And Jesus went over to comfort the woman, telling her, "Go, and sin no more" (see John 8).

Religion

A Public Relations Campaign for God

When I was young I had a friend whose father was the pastor at a Methodist church. I grew up Baptist. I remember thinking my friend had it all wrong, and I wondered if he was even a Christian. His father was a terrific man, very intelligent and soft-spoken and tall as a building, with big hands and a deep voice that spoke the sort of encouragement you believed. And even though he spoke encouragement, I remember feeling very sorry for him because he had been misled, somewhere way back, perhaps in seminary, and that had made him grow up to become a Methodist instead of a Baptist. I thought it was a crying shame. And at the time I didn't even know what it was a Baptist believed that a Methodist didn't; I only knew we were right and they were wrong.

I suppose believing we were right and they were wrong gave me a feeling of superiority over my Methodist friends. It all sounds so innocent until you realize whatever evil thing it was that caused me to believe Baptists are better than Methodists is the same evil thing that has Jews killing Palestinians rather than talking to them, and for that matter, Palestinians killing Jews rather than engaging in an important conversation about land and history and peace. It makes you wonder how many of the ideas we believe are the result of our being taught them, and we now defend them as a position of our egos.

Of course I think the thing about Methodists being wrong is silly now, now that I have met so many people from so many different theological backgrounds who have a deep respect and love for Jesus, and so many people from so many theological backgrounds who don't.

The truth is, many of us go around thinking we are right about everything. When God was in the Garden, I'll bet Adam and Eve didn't know what it felt like to want to be right. I'll bet they felt right all the time, and I'll bet it had nothing to do with *what* they knew and everything to do with *who* they knew, as though whatever it was inside them that said they didn't think right or feel right or believe right was activated only after God left. I'll bet they never said anything like *I told you so.*

If you think about it, right and wrong aren't even people, they are ideas, philosophical equations and that sort of thing, and so it is funny that anybody would think they are right in the first place. I suppose what we really mean when we say we are right is that something out there in the soup of ideas is right, and we simply agree with whatever it is the soup is saying. But this doesn't have anything to do with our rightness or wrongness; it just means we can read.

I'm not trying to be a relativist by any means, I am only saying a person is not right or wrong; a person is just a body and a brain and a soul. And even if a person subscribes to a certain take on life he feels is the right take, it's not because he had a lot to do with it. If we grew up in Christian homes and heard about Jesus all our lives, we shouldn't believe we arrived at these theological positions through an independent navigation of our minds. We were just going with the flow, and there isn't any genius in going with the flow. Show me a guy who was molested by a minister and still loves Jesus, and I'll show you a genius. The stuff that guy would have had to think through in order to arrive at an affection for God is nothing short of miraculous.

As for me, I'm somebody who repeats what I was taught in Sunday school using fancier language. It may pay the rent, but it isn't original thought.

—

And yet it is amazing how I can take these beautiful things Jesus told me, this skeleton of the human story He explains in narrative and poetry, and turn it around as though I wrote it on the back of a napkin at Denny's in a moment of inspiration.

Shouldn't I be grateful that God showed this stuff to me rather than connecting the theology to my identity and then using it to distinguish myself from *inferiors* who haven't figured it out?

I had dinner with a friend down south recently who didn't know Christ and I invited a pastor along, hoping the conversation might turn to Jesus. When my pastor friend discovered my other friend wasn't a Christian, he asked a question I thought was very sad. He asked if my other friend had ever thought Christians were right.

I confess, the question took me aback. I can conceive a number of questions more inviting than whether or not Christians are right. Right about what? The Crusades? Republican policies? Televangelists?

Asking whether my friend thought Christians were right was really a question about the questioner and his identity, not about God. My pastor friend was asking my other friend to admit we were right and he was wrong—his journey was wrong, his experience was wrong, his heart was wrong, his mind was wrong. He was asking my friend to join our party in the lifeboat. That's a lot to ask of a guy. The sad part of this story is, my friend who isn't a Christian was hurt and politely changed the subject, and we haven't talked about God since. I apologized to him later, and, unfortunately, the subject has yet to come back up.

The ever-overquoted C. S. Lewis said it this way in his book *Mere Christianity:* "Most of us are not really approaching the subject in order to find out what Christianity says: We are approaching it in the hope of finding support from Christianity for the views of our own party. We are looking for an ally where we are offered either a Master or—a Judge."

And that's the thing about being religious; it isn't this safe place in the soul you can go, it has just as many booby traps as any other thing you can get yourself into. It's a bloody brothel, in fact. Jesus even says there will be people who will heal other people, but when they die He is going to say He didn't *know* them. It is somewhat amazing to me, once again, that all of Christianity, all our grids and mathematics and truths and different groups subscribing to different theological ideas, boils down to our *knowing* Jesus and His *knowing* us.

Apart from the booby trap of getting redemption from believing we are right and they are wrong, there is the booby trap of believing we gain access to God by knowing a lot of religious information.

Rather than Scripture serving as the text that explains God, it becomes a puzzle by which we test our knowledge against our friends', and the views by which we distinguish superiors from inferiors. It is as though we believe that when we die, Alex Trebeck will be standing at the gates of heaven to lead us in a mad round of religious Jeopardy: *I'll take Calvinism for a seat next to Christ, Alex.*

In the context of my relationship with God, I know the temptation to bank on knowledge all too well. It is true that you can get a little buzz off knowing a couple of smart theological ideas. My friend Ross is a former seminary professor, and we were driving back from lunch one afternoon and I was telling him what I thought about a particular passage of Scripture, really going off about it as though I were the first of all men to understand what it meant. When I stopped to allow Ross space to tell me how smart I was, he just sat there in silence. "What do you think, Ross?" I asked. "Well," he said quietly, "I think knowledge puffs up."

Scripture says the nature of sin is deceptive, so deceptive that a person's mind can be carried away, and he will have no idea he has become something arrogant and proud and offensive until one of his friends slaps him on the back of the head.

And I wonder about that, about how much of my faith I apply in a personal way, deep down in my heart on the level where I actually mean things. I know there are selfish motives mixed with my faith, that this community of faith is the jury of peers and they applaud when I know a lot of fancy theological stuff, and that can really screw a guy up. I learn more and get more applause and learn more and get even more applause. To describe people like me, Jesus would use the word *hypocrite*, which, at the time, was a term used to describe Greek actors. Jesus, in fact, is thought to be the first person to coin the phrase. Those on the scene must have found the similarities quite humorous—the exaggerated language, the proud countenances, the broad and showy mannerisms. How obvious it must have been to Jesus that this was all a sham. *They don't even know Me,* He must have thought. *They don't even know My Father.*

Eugene Peterson translates Paul's disdain for religious leaders of the day rather scathingly:

> I'm giving nobody grounds for lumping me in with those money-grubbing "preachers," vaunting themselves as something special. They're a sorry bunch—pseudo-apostles, lying preachers, crooked workers—posing as Christ's agents but sham to the core. And no wonder! Satan does it all the time, dressing up as a beautiful angel of light. So it shouldn't surprise us when his servants masquerade as servants of God. But they're not getting by with anything. They'll pay for it in the end.
>
> (2 Cor. 11:12–15 THE MESSAGE)

I want to confess something I don't talk about very often. I tell you this only because as I write, it is late and the house is quiet and I feel a little sentimental.

What I want to say is this: I could very easily have become one of those guys Paul is talking about. It is truly an amazing feeling to stand in front of a crowd and deliver a great sermon, or to hang around after a reading and sign books. I've never been very good at anything, so the only thing people have ever praised me for is writing and speaking. I'm not saying that accepting people's praise for doing what God calls you to do is wrong, I am only saying I understand how it could become a replacement for the favor of God, the favor that comes for free, for no reason, unearned. What good is that in the lifeboat? It's almost like quitting.

The tough thing about Christian spirituality is, you have to mean things. You can't just go through the motions or act religious for the wrong reasons.

It's crazy, isn't it? It's crazy because, as I've suggested all along, this thing is a thing of the heart. It's intimacy with Christ, wrestling with the truth of the soul rather than a dog and pony show in the center ring of a circus.

Jesus, by initiating what we call Communion, disciplines such as fasting, and the sacrament of baptism, takes the spiritual disciplines from the abstract realm of religion and places them within the meaningful realm of relationship. Fasting is mourning Him, baptism is identifying with Him, Communion is remembering Him. It all comes down to our thoughts and feelings and faith in Him. If our minds are not on Christ and we treat Communion like a little religious pill or baptism like a woo-woo bath or we fast to feel some kind of pain about our sacrifice, the significance is gone. It is the trick of Satan to get us to go through religious motions divorced of their relational significance. It is the trick of Satan to get us to perform religious actions without *meaning* them.

After all, if we are going through religious motions to get people to think of us as religious, praise us, and all that, we are receiving our false redemption from a bunch of people who are going to be dead in fifty years. This is a shabby replacement for an eternal God.

I've a friend who has a leather-bound day planner, and on an inside page of the planner there is a space for facts about a spouse: her dress size, her favorite foods, her favorite music. Amazingly, this is not a page my friend created on a blank sheet of paper;

rather, he bought it from the company that makes the time-management system. We laughed together at the oddity of the idea of trying to calculate, plan, and structure knowledge that would be meaningful to a woman only if her husband knew it as a consequence of his love. The whole point of intimacy is that you want to know things, random facts; you are driven to them because this woman has *taken you captive*, not that you would willfully write them down as a matter of discipline. Imagine calling your wife to tell her you love her and then hanging up the phone to check off the action on your to-do list. I don't think she would be pleased in the slightest. She would probably rather not have received a call at all. No, in romance, as in spirituality, your motives have to be selfless, driven from an authentic love for the other person.

Lately I have been thinking about the verse in Scripture that says to work out your salvation in fear and trembling (see Phil. 2:12). I take this to mean salvation isn't something you go around feeling sure of, the way you might if you had completed a to-do list. I take this to mean working out our salvation involves a very careful searching of the heart, asking time and again what we really mean by attending church, what we really mean by reading the Bible, what we really mean when we worship God.

It bears repeating that the last conversation John reported Jesus having was with Peter, asking three times if Peter loves Him, and defining that love's manifestation as service to the people in the church, working itself out in love for others. And it also bears repeating that Jesus told the Pharisees the greatest commandment was to love the Lord your God with all your heart, soul, mind, and strength. I would think the Pharisees of the day would have dismissed this as a kind of affective theology, mushy talk, not very rational, and yet the whole time Jesus was extending an invitation to a spiritual marriage, our oneness with Him allowing God to see us in Christ's righteousness rather than our own. It would be most tragic for a person to know everything about God, but not God; to know all about the rules of spiritual marriage, but never walk the aisle.

At the time of Martin Luther, the church was building sanctuaries by selling bricks to people in exchange for indulgences. If a person bought a brick, they would be forgiven a few more sins or help a loved one out of purgatory. Because people couldn't read, and there weren't very many copies of the Bible floating around anyway, religious leaders used the threat of hell and God's wrath to manipulate the masses. But, as I mentioned earlier, when Luther read a copy of the Bible for himself, he began a reformation against this kind of crap. It makes you wonder how amazed he was when he first read the words of Christ in the book of Matthew, words about people who would try to distort relational truth and turn it into propositional truth for their own gain: "Instead of giving you God's Law as food and drink by which you can banquet on God," Jesus begins, talking about the Pharisees,

> They package it in bundles of rules, loading you down like pack animals. They seem to take pleasure in watching you stagger under these loads, and wouldn't think of lifting a finger to help. Their lives are perpetual fashion shows, embroidered prayer shawls one day and flowery prayers the next. They love to sit at the head table at church dinners, basking in the most prominent positions, preening in the radiance of public flattery, receiving honorary degrees, and getting called "Doctor" and "Reverend."
>
> Don't let people do that to you, put you on a pedestal like

> that. You all have a single Teacher, and you are all classmates. Don't set people up as experts over your life, letting them tell you what to do. Save that authority for God; let him tell you what to do. No one else should carry the title of "Father"; you have only one Father, and he's in heaven. And don't let people maneuver you into taking charge of them. There is only one Life-Leader for you and them—Christ.
>
> (Matt. 23:4–10 THE MESSAGE)

I know it's tempting to believe if we will walk through ten steps or listen to only a certain kind of music or pray in a certain way and for a certain number of days then we will find favor with God, but we won't. The formulas, I understand, were created by their authors to help us, but they do more hindering than helping. If we trust in a formula, if we trust in steps, we are not trusting in God. Formulas, while helping us organize our faith, also tempt us to trust in them rather than in God. In my own faith journey, I have disregarded formulas entirely.

There are many religions, and many religious sects within the faith of Christianity. Do I believe some are more scripturally faithful than others? *Yes.* But none of them matter in the slightest if formulas replace a personal relationship with Jesus. He is the authority we need. He is the God we must cling to for salvation. And He is a Person, not a list of ideas, not a theology.

The Danger of Marketing the Formulas

It is true that people need Jesus, not religion. And yet at times I am concerned our most passionate missionary endeavors are more concerned with redeeming our identity as Christians within the lifeboat than with presenting Jesus to a world looking for a God.

As my pastor friend down south revealed in his question to my lost friend, it often seems what we really want is for people who are not Christians to think we are valid, or Christianity is valid, rather than showing them Jesus, who won't act as a balm for their wounds.

I've a friend named Deacon, for instance, who attended a church here in Oregon that boasted a thriving youth ministry. My friend, who is a ridiculously intelligent physicist, told me that he was involved in this youth ministry when he was in high school. The strategy of the youth ministry, he said, was to recruit the most popular students from each of the local schools, knowing that if the popular students came, everybody else would follow. Because of this, youth ministers aggressively pursued jocks and cheerleaders with events such as slam-dunk contests and pizza feeds. The strategy, of course, worked, and hundreds of kids came, following the cheerleaders and jocks. Each year this ministry would divide the massive youth group into teams of about ten students, and the teams competed against one another for a series of weeks in games—stuff like three-legged races and that sort of thing. Bands were brought in, and speakers came and gave talks about how a person can be cool and still be a follower of Jesus. Each week the intensity would grow as teams competed for points toward first, second, and third places. And each year, as the winning team was announced, students would scream and cheer as the winning team, most often a team with a lot of jocks and cool kids, came up and received their trophy.

My friend told me, laughingly, that when he was in high school he was scrawny, awkward, and definitely not the sort of kid the ministry prized. And not only was he not one of the popular kids, but there weren't any popular kids on his team. "We were really a bunch of nerds," he said. And yet somehow, Deacon told me, their team managed to stay neck and neck in the points.

"I don't know how we did it," he said. "There wasn't a jock among us. But on the last night, there we were toward the top of the pack. And I remember thinking about how awesome it would be to win the event. Every year the team that won was ushered up front and people went nuts. I could just feel it, you know, walking up there to get the trophy with all these cool kids, all these jocks and cheerleaders finally noticing that I existed."

"So what happened?" I asked.

"Well," Deacon continued, "the last night came around, and we knew we were in the running. We competed hard, harder than any of us had ever competed before, and because the games were so screwy, you know, run to the other side of the gym and put your head on the end of a baseball bat and spin around and then come back, that sort of thing, the fact none of us were athletes hardly affected us. Anybody can turn around and get dizzy. But it was still close, and when the whole thing was done, we didn't know whether we had won. There were a couple other teams that were also close."

"So did you win?" I asked, rather sucked into the story, hoping, quite honestly, that a team of misfits would come out ahead.

"I'm getting there," Deacon continued. "So the youth leaders left the room and started calculating the scores, you know, and all of the teams were cheering, kind of yelling at one another in unison, and my team was so nervous that we kind of sat there in silence. And then finally, after what seemed like an eternity, the youth leaders came back into the room. They gathered everybody around in a big semicircle and grabbed the trophy and talked about how close it all was, and everybody was still kind of cheering so they had to quiet everybody down, and then the head youth pastor told us all to give a drum roll, you know, like pat our legs and the floor and the place was going nuts with this drum roll. And then he yelled the name of *our* team into the microphone. We had won. I couldn't believe it, but we actually won the thing." When Deacon delivered these last lines, he said them softly, almost as though he were ashamed.

"But you won, Deacon. That's great," I said.

"Yeah, it was great, but it was also one of the most humiliating nights of my life."

"What are you talking about?"

"Well, when the youth pastor called our team's name, the place more or less went silent. I mean, some people were cheering, but as we stood up and they realized who we were, they all went quiet. It was as though they weren't sure whether it was right to cheer for us or not. The place had been so geared around jocks and cheerleaders, they weren't sure if our winning was a good thing. I never felt like such a loser in my life."

And of course I told Deacon what he already knew, that this kind of thing was wrong, that Jesus went directly to those who were marginalized, not showing partiality at all. Deacon said he knew that, and he assured me he was over it, but I wondered. I wondered because I grew up a misfit, too, and while the youth ministry I attended when I was a kid was a safe haven for misfits, I can't imagine being able to get over that moment as quickly as Deacon did. I can't imagine not having stayed up at night wondering if God would feel the same way about me as the kids in the lifeboat.

I began to wonder if what we were really doing in evangelical circles, then, had more to do with redeeming ourselves to culture than it did with showing Jesus to a hurting world, a world literally filled with outcasts.

Not long after Deacon told me that story, I was in a record shop with a friend who was also in ministry. And we were having this same conversation, and I was saying that I think, as Christians, we might be obsessed with whether or not we appear *cool* to the world. My friend disagreed and talked about all the ministries that minister to the outcasts; how if it weren't for the church, many people would go hungry, and many people would die lonely.

"That's true," I said to my friend. "But let's try a little experiment." I looked out over the record store, a mass-market chain store that must have housed ten thousand CDs, and I asked him to go into the racks and find one ugly person on the cover of a record.

"Do what?" my friend asked.

"You know, find an ugly person."

"Okay," my friend said reluctantly, and with that he walked into the aisle and started thumbing through the discs.

"What about this one?" he said, holding up a compact disc with a dorky-looking guy holding an acoustic guitar, the letters of the type looking like something printed in the sixties, but the picture very much modern.

"Easy enough, isn't it?" I asked.

"Yeah, sure," he said sarcastically. But the reason I had asked him to do this was because I knew our next stop would be a large Christian bookstore here in Portland, a bookstore that has an entire room devoted to music. We were heading over there to pick up a case of books we had ordered. When we arrived at the store, I asked my friend to come to the music room with me and I asked him to do the same thing, to find a record with an ugly person on the cover.

"I see what you're getting at," he said with a smile. And he started walking down the aisle. I went with him and both of us thumbed through the discs, picking out covers and showing them to each other, but none of the artists even slightly passed for ugly.

We spent about twenty minutes looking though the records but came up with nothing. We literally couldn't find one record cover with an ugly person on it. You can try the same experiment if you like. And I don't mean any of this to say that good-looking people are bad. I would actually like to be a good-looking person one day. I am only saying we are, perhaps, even more obsessed, in the church, with the stuff culture is obsessed with. We are hardly providing an alternative worldview. The mantra seems to be "Trust in Jesus! He will redeem you to the world."

The examples get worse. A friend told me recently he volunteered at a church only a mile from my house. This is a large church with a successful television ministry. He said his job was to usher people to their seats, and that after he had been on the job for a while, he was asked to put some of the more "pleasant-looking people" on the front rows as these people were more likely to be caught in the picture when the camera pulled out on the audience, or when the preacher walked down from the stage to make a point.

I assure you, I am not making this up.

And please don't misunderstand me. There are very few churches like this, but as a Christian community, if Paul or Peter or whoever were to write a letter to us, I think this business of showing favoritism and being obsessed with the way we market our faith might come up.

The second chapter of the book of James tells us, specifically, not to take a wealthy person and seat him in a place of honor and leave a poor person in the back. I take this to mean that in church, the rules of the lifeboat don't apply, that church is a refuge, where the kingdom of God is emulated, not mocked.

I realize by making these statements, I will cause some to think I don't like the church, or I don't like religion. This isn't the case. If religion helps in our relationship with God, and it does, that's great, but if it is how we check stuff off a to-do list, or if it is the identity we defend in the lifeboat, or if our idea of evangelism is redeeming the image of Christianity, and not displaying the economy of the kingdom on earth, then it is worthless. I don't have any reservations about saying that.

That said, I know there are also some people who will want to lump Christians into a single category as hypocrites and jerks, and certainly I have presented this side of the argument, but I've done so only in warning, as Paul did, as James did, and as Jesus did. But I also have to tell you that some of the most beautiful people I have ever met have been Christians. Walk into most churches and you will find a safe haven, a refuge.

As a guy who grew up something of a misfit, I can assure you few would have loved me were it not for my local church. When *Jesus* gets inside somebody, the first thing that starts happening is the person starts loving people regardless of their race, their socioeconomic status, or their looks. And, unfortunately, the people whom Jesus gets inside are at churches, along with the people who are marketing the formulas.

But I have been loved by people who know Jesus. And I don't know that there is any greater love than the love from those who have been touched by the Messiah. I do hope you get to meet one of these people someday and feel the kind of love I am talking about. And as for the others, our job isn't to judge them, but to love them. Jesus will judge them enough for all of us. We all are works in progress, we all are learning that the lifeboat mentality is sin, but it takes time. And bitterness is only a manifestation of the game.

Religion is a big, beautiful, ugly thing. I read recently where Augustine said, "The church is a whore and it is my mother." And for reasons I don't understand, Jesus loves the church. And I suppose He loves the church with the same strength of character He displays in His love for me. Sometimes it is difficult to know which is the greater miracle.

FOURTEEN

The Gospel of Jesus

Why William Shakespeare Was a Prophet

After attending the writers' seminar, the one that taught us to present self-help arguments in three-step formulas, and after I tried to write one myself, having looked through Scripture to find anything like a self-help formula, and after having found nothing, nothing appealing anyway, I started wondering exactly how a person would explain the gospel of Jesus. Let's say you had a friend like Omar who was wondering, and you no longer believed the gospel could be presented accurately using a step-by-step guide with all the beauty of blender instructions, what exactly would you say?

And I supposed what you would have to do would be to tell a bunch of stories. You could explain the basics in propositional speak, but to get to the heart of the thing you would have to tell a bunch of stories. After all, this is what God does in Scripture. And it's real-life stuff, too, as though He interacted with humanity to create allegories inside the actual story, so that the living allegories would point outward, toward what the big story is about. Take the book of Job, for instance. Some would say the book of Job is about pain, that hidden inside the story are secret steps to take when you happen to be dealing with pain. I don't think this is true, exactly. I think the book of Job is a story about *life*, and there aren't any secret steps in it at all.

My friend John MacMurray tells me the first book written in the Bible is the book of Job. Moses wrote Job before he wrote Genesis, some scholars agree, and so the first thing God wanted to communicate to mankind was that life is hard, and there is pain, great pain in life, and yet the answer to this pain, or the cure for this pain, is not given in explanation; rather, God offers to this pain, or this life experience, Himself. Not steps, not an understanding, not a philosophy, but Himself. I take this to mean the first thing God wanted to communicate to humanity was that He was God, He was very large and in control, storing snow in Kansas, stopping waves at a certain point on the beach, causing clouds to carry rain, causing wind to race down imaginary hills of barometric pressure, and that if He could do all this, then He could be trusted, and that, perhaps, this would help us through our lives. And so from the beginning, from the very first story told in Scripture, God presents life, as it is, without escape, with only Himself to cling to. It worked for Job, after all, because even before God healed him and even before God returned his wealth and even while Job was sitting by a fire picking scabs from his wounds and mourning his family, he would respond to the whirlwind God spoke through by saying, *All this is too wonderful for me.*

Another story God tells is of Hosea. This is a story God actually *made* happen by telling Hosea, His prophet, to marry and have children with a whore. It's a terribly painful story, to be honest, thick with love and deception, with the pain and heartache of a man who loves a woman purely and a woman who opens her legs at the drop of a hat. She has issues, to be sure, but Hosea loves her through those issues, sees her beauty, is mesmerized by her beauty and the hope of a love with her. His love is unrelenting, pure as diamonds.

It's real-life stuff, blood and tears, and in it is all the introduction we need to the love of God, identifying ourselves with this prostitute who runs from the only one who really cares about her. In this story, God explains to us the great dynamic that is taking place in the universe, the great story unfolding in the annals of humanity. God never could have said any of this with a formula. God could not have explained this by presenting a few steps, a few principles of spiritual growth. God wanted Hosea to experience this, and He wanted it written down for all of time, because He wanted humanity to know how He feels. And yet Hosea is another book largely ignored because it has nothing to help us achieve the American dream, unless, of course, we use it as instructions for sleeping around.

It strikes me, even as I type this, how distant and far our formulaic methodology is from the artful, narrative sort of methodology used to explain God in Scripture. It makes you wonder whether we can even get to the truth of our theology unless it is presented in the sort of methodology Scripture uses. It makes you wonder if all our time spent making lists would be better spent painting or writing or singing or learning to speak stories. Sometimes I feel as though the church has a kind of pity for Scripture, always having to come behind it and explain everything, put everything into actionable steps, acronyms, and hidden secrets, as though the original writers, and for that matter the Holy Spirit who worked in the lives of the original writers, were a bunch of illiterate hillbillies. I don't think they were illiterate hillbillies, and I think the methodology God used to explain His truth is quite superior.

What I mean by this is I feel my life is a story, more than a list; I feel this blood slipping through my veins and these chemicals in my brain telling me I am hungry or lonely, sad or angry, in love or despondent. And I don't feel that a list could ever explain the complexity of all this beauty, all this sun and moon, this smell of coming rain, the beautiful mysteries of women, or the truck-like complexity of men. It seems nearly heresy to explain the gospel of Jesus, this message an infinitely complex God has delivered to an infinitely complex humanity, in bullet points. How amazing is it that Christ would explain that to be His followers we must eat His flesh and drink His blood, and that He is the Bridegroom and we are the bride, and that we will be unified with Him in His death, and that we will live forever with Him in glory.

—

Do you know where I found what I believe is the most beautiful explanation for the gospel of Jesus ever presented? It's been under our noses for hundreds of years, right there in the most famous scene in all of English literature. You've probably rented the movie, and you studied it in high school. You may even have some of the lines memorized, or you might have played a character in its performance onstage. The greatest art I've seen that explains how beautiful it is to cast our hope for redemption upon Christ is the balcony scene in *Romeo and Juliet.*

I confess, the first time I saw the play I didn't think much of it; it seemed just the story of two kids who, rather stupidly, killed themselves over a misunderstanding about some poison, but a couple of years ago I got to thinking about the play again and stayed up late a bunch of nights in a row and read it over and over, always coming to the balcony scene and wondering why exactly Shakespeare would word the dialogue the way he did. I think you will find the wording quite peculiar.

At the beginning of the play, Romeo thinks he is in love with a girl named Rosaline, but he sees Juliet at a party and immediately falls in love with her, understanding his previous love for Rosaline as something formulaic and invented, something to make him *feel* he is in love rather than actually *being* in love. Mercutio, in fact, would criticize Romeo's affection for Rosaline, saying "he loves by numbers." Immediately, however, when his eyes fall across Juliet, Romeo feels an instant love only the poets understand. They meet at a party, a party Romeo was not invited to, a party he and his friends have crashed, and he cannot take his eyes from this remarkable woman, a child of the Capulets. It becomes obvious that Juliet has, as Shakespeare would say elsewhere, "taken prisoner the wild motion of Romeo's eye." And when Romeo and his friends leave the party, the young Montague sneaks away from his friends and moves stealthily back toward the Capulet home. His friends chastise him for such erratic behavior, to which Romeo responds, under his breath, "He jests at scars, that never felt a wound."

Romeo then crawls over the wall into the Capulets' courtyard and stands beneath Juliet's balcony, quietly so as to not disrupt the Capulet house because Romeo, a Montague, is despised by the Capulets, as a feud exists between the two families, which, according to the prince of Verona, was "bred of airy words," that is, had come from nothing. And here, in the Capulet courtyard, Romeo speaks the now famous lines:

But, soft! what light through yonder window breaks?
It is the east, and Juliet is the sun!
Arise fair sun and kill the envious moon,
Who is already sick and pale with grief,
That thou her maid art far more fair than she.

In referring to Juliet as the sun, and comparing her brightness to that of the moon, Romeo is contrasting her beauty against that of Rosaline, for whom, earlier in the play, he used lunar imagery.

The scene indicates not only Romeo's preference for Juliet over Rosaline but also his willingness to consider a lover who would disrupt his life, the obvious enmity between the two families having been established from scene one. Not only this, but in comparing his love for Juliet to his previous feelings for Rosaline, Romeo is comparing this compulsory love he feels for Juliet to that of the formulaic, Petrarchan feelings he experienced for Rosaline.

Petrarch was a fourteenth-century Italian poet who wrote endlessly of his love for a woman named Laura. Petrarch believed love had rules, that one must be careful in the ways of it, guarding emotion and investing, rather, in a sort of mathematical approach to interacting with women. Mercutio, early in the play, compares Romeo to Petrarch, and the comment is intended as an insult. Shakespeare pays homage to Petrarch by having Romeo speak of Rosaline in iambic pentameter, the sort of rigid rhyme employed by Petrarch himself, and switches to free verse when causing Romeo to speak of Juliet. This would indicate Romeo's feelings for Juliet are sincere, while his feelings for Rosaline had been contrived. Later in the play, in fact, Juliet counsels Romeo to not speak to her in the rigid verse he had used in his less-authentic expressions toward Rosaline, and return to the free verse she had come to associate with his feelings for her.

In this scene, Juliet may be considered the Bard's Christ figure, and Romeo the embodiment of the church, thus presenting Shakespeare's opinion of a Christian conversion experience. I realize it sounds far-fetched, and that I may be reading theology into a play that is simply a love story, but upon closer examination we see Shakespeare borrowing exclusively from the themes of

Christ's love for the church, even going so far as to leave his own story, that of Romeo's wanting of Juliet, to enter completely into the unique complexities of Christ's interaction with the church. You will have to remember that at the time of Shakespeare's popularity, everybody had an opinion about salvation. Many scholars believe the enmity between the Montagues and Capulets, for example, represented the tension between Protestants and Catholics. This view holds merit because at the time Shakespeare wrote the play, tension between the Protestants and Catholics had risen to a fever pitch on the streets outside the poet's home. Shakespeare was not writing in twenty-first-century America, where religion and state are separated and great caution is taken to keep opinions about the heavens within personal fences; rather, opinions regarding theology burned bright as flags. A brief history lesson might help us understand the poet's intent with the scene in the Capulet courtyard.

William Shakespeare was born not more than a century after the invention of the printing press, perhaps the most important invention of all time, greater in shaping culture than the Internet. The streets of London were alive with new buzz at the time Shakespeare began writing plays. People were learning how to read, and because of this, nothing in history would be the same. The most dramatic changes in the social landscape stemmed from people's access to the Bible. Before the printing press, the universal church had distorted Scripture in an effort to control communities and amass wealth and power. As mentioned in a previous chapter, great cathedrals were being built throughout Europe from the profits of indulgences.

Luther's writings, then, along with those of John Calvin, would begin the Protestant (protesters) Reformation, which had dramatic implications in Shakespeare's London only thirty or so years later.

In England, the Reformation did not gain power until Henry VIII divorced his wife, which earned him an excommunication from the pope. Parliament then reacted to the pope by passing the Act of Supremacy, which made the king head of the church in England. Henry VIII was then succeeded by Edward VI, a ten-year-old boy, whose short six-year reign would allow the Anglican church to grow and begin its persecution of the Catholics. A sickly Edward VI died in 1553 and was replaced by his half-sister Mary, who earned the name Bloody Mary by upholding her Catholic roots, turning the tide on Protestants and executing them in large numbers. Mary's successor, Elizabeth, would comply with her half-sister's Catholic leanings while Mary was alive, but on her succession would once again restore Protestantism to the throne. In this way, England's throne passed from Protestantism to Catholicism and back to Protestantism in the span of a single decade, each change bringing with it the slaughter of thousands.

Shakespeare was born and worked during the reign of Elizabeth. This set him in an England in which the religious tension had yet to subside. Not unlike the tension that exists today in Northern Ireland, these two groups were at odds, their faith connected to their ideas about God and heaven, their political leanings, and their identities. It makes a great deal of sense then that from the struggle of Catholics against Protestants and Protestants against Catholics, Shakespeare may have molded his idea of a tension between the Montagues and Capulets. It is true the story of Romeo and Juliet existed many years before Shakespeare adapted it for the stage, but the poet may have borrowed from the tension on the street to color the tension between the two families. Indeed, with the tension as high as it was at the time, it is doubtful the argument did not color the text.

Reading the balcony scene through the lens of an Elizabethan audience reveals what I think is a powerful double entendre, one that suggests not only a sort of negotiation of love between Juliet and Romeo, but a kind of invitation from Christ to the church, to you and me, walking us, as it were, on the heart path a person would need to traffic in order to know Christ and be saved from his broken nature. Without question, the precepts Juliet presents to Romeo may be broken down as identical matches of the theology John Calvin penned not too many years before Shakespeare wrote the play. And it is these principles set in the context of a dramatic love story that truly bring the implications of the gospel of Jesus to life.

The Gospel of Jesus

Again, Romeo is standing beneath Juliet's balcony, having wished for her to step onto her perch above the courtyard, bright as the sun, putting an end to the moon, when his wish is granted. Juliet slips out the doors of her bedroom, looks out on the evening with a sigh, and leans her gentle frame against the railing. Romeo is silent beneath her beauty when Juliet speaks:

> *O Romeo, Romeo! wherefore art thou Romeo?*
> *Deny thy father, and refuse thy name;*
> *Or, if thou wilt not, be but sworn my love,*
> *And I'll no longer be a Capulet.*

In these lines Juliet is expressing her love for Romeo, but also stating her understanding that the two shall never be one as long as he is called a Montague and she is called a Capulet. In a monologue Juliet will soon deliver, asking, "What's in a name? that which we call a rose by any other name would smell as sweet," the playwright borrows from the trouble of man's nature and the duality of his goodness and his brokenness, one being compatible with a relationship with God, and the other set in enmity, unable to mingle with the pure nature of God. Juliet asks Romeo to doff, or disavow, his name, and if he won't, then swear his love, and she will no longer be a Capulet. This means the two of them will have to meet within some other name, and for allegorical purposes (though it's questionable whether Shakespeare intended this much), within some other nature. In the context of the story of Romeo and Juliet, this idea makes complete sense. The two want to be together, but their names keep them apart, so Juliet asks Romeo to throw off his name so the two may unite.

It struck me as I read these lines, however, that no less of a proposition would be made by Christ in the Gospel of Luke:

> Now great multitudes went with Him. And He turned and said to them, "If anyone comes to Me and does not hate his father and mother, wife and children, brothers and sisters, yes, and his own life also, he cannot be My disciple." (14:25–26 NKJV)

I used to read this passage and think of Jesus as difficult and strict and, to be honest, I didn't like Him for saying it. But when I saw it in the context of the balcony scene of *Romeo and Juliet,* the same ideas being expressed in an effort for two people to unite, it became something different, and I confess, I wouldn't want the language to be any less strict. Language less strict might suggest love less pure. True love, love in its highest form, must cost the participants everything. Both parties would have to be willing to give up everything in order to have each other.

In exchange for what Scripture calls repentance, by renouncing our natures, by admitting our own brokenness, we may take all of Christ, identifying ourselves with His righteousness.

We see this beautifully portrayed in the words of Juliet, who, after musing about Romeo's dual nature, delivers the thrust of her invitation:

> *Romeo, doff thy name,*
> *And for that name, which is no part of thee,*
> *Take all myself.*

Should Romeo take Juliet up on her proposition, he will not gain love for love's sake, but rather Juliet herself. This idea is all biblical but the stuff of poets. The playwright understood that Christ's invitation was not an offer of heaven or mansions or money; it was, rather, Himself. In multiple contexts Jesus claims we shall be one with Him even as He and the disciples are one and the Trinity before them are One. Just as, if a wife travels away from her family on business, the family feels her absence in their hearts, so we are to have this kind of oneness with Christ. And just as a sheep knows the voice of its shepherd, so are we to know the voice of Christ, and just as a lost child in a store feels fear and pain in his parent's absence, so we are to feel disoriented in the absence of God, and comforted in our relationship with Jesus. This, I believe, is what the Bible means when it speaks of our oneness: It isn't a technicality, it is an actual relationship.

Romeo hears these words from Juliet and understands the implications of her invitation. He believes that if he denies his name, she shall deliver herself and the two shall become one. And this is where Shakespeare leaves the parallel elements of love story and picks up the pen of Calvin. Romeo, speaking to Juliet, says:

> *I take thee at thy word.*
> *Call me but love, and I'll be new baptiz'd;*
> *Henceforth I never will be Romeo.*

Here Romeo indicates he believes what Juliet is saying is true. This confession of belief is crucial to Shakespeare's understanding of the proper recipient of love. There can be no doubting, no mistrust; one must have complete faith in the other that nothing is being held back. In our spirituality, we see nothing different. No less than two hundred times Scripture speaks of the importance of belief. "I take thee at thy word," Romeo says, meaning he believes Juliet's invitation, that she will do what she says she will do. Anything less than this complete trust from Romeo would not be love, anything less than pure trust would be a kind of careful negotiation. And careful negotiation isn't love. A person must be willing to be dashed on the rocks or made the fool in exchange for a relationship in order for pure love to take place. And in our spirituality, anything less indicates a questioning of God's character.

These ideas played out in the pages of Scripture would have Christ asking that we "follow" Him, a term that in the Greek would also indicate a clinging to Him or imitation of Him. Christ, in short, asks us to give everything, all our false redemption in the lifeboat, all our false ideas about who God is, all our trust in something other than God to redeem us. In so doing, we die to our broken natures in exchange for His perfect nature, and find a unification with Him that will allow God to see us as one, just as a husband is one with a wife.

And great attention must be given to Romeo's response to Juliet. Romeo does not say yes, that he will change his name; rather, he understands that he has no power to change his nature, and he looks to Juliet and submits all power to her. Romeo says: "Call me but love, and I'll be new baptiz'd."

If Romeo is to be made new, if his name is to be changed, it will not be of his own doing. He understands he has no ability to change his own name, that it will not be by an act of his own will that his nature is made new; rather, it will be on the whim and wish of Juliet. If she calls him love, then he will be called love, both his name and his nature changed, made new.

Indeed, a few lines later Juliet will call to Romeo, and Romeo will remind his muse that his name has been changed, and he will no longer answer to Romeo.

In our spirituality the idea is no less critical. Paul would indicate we have no ability to do good on our own. Now certainly we have the ability to do good things, to do nice things for people and even for God, but Paul spoke of a problem at the very core of our nature, that even our desire to submit to God, a good desire indeed, would have to be stimulated by God Himself. We are in the lifeboat, as it were, Children of Chernobyl. In this way, Romeo, as well as the whore that is the church of God, bends itself before its muse in complete submission, asking only God, who has given Himself, to invite her into this dramatic story of love, passion, and union. The strength is all His, and the gift is all ours.

—

In this beautiful way William Shakespeare weaves the intricate complexities of the love relationship between God and the church into the context of narrative, and in so doing creates a scene that would not be eclipsed by ten million stories told since. When we read the balcony scene of *Romeo and Juliet*, we understand intrinsically that what is being negotiated is love, and that the poet has explained the mysterious complexities of this negotiation perfectly. Everything is at stake, and everything must be given to achieve the unity of souls.

And yet the poet is not finished. The agreement has been made between Romeo and Juliet, but they are far from unified. In any other story, the credits would roll, but Shakespeare has more to teach us, and the true beauty is yet to come.

Unity in Death

In the pages of Scripture the desire for the afterlife does not involve gaining a kind of euphoria over troubles, exactly, but rather concerns the opportunity to be with God. The euphoria over troubles comes as an afterthought, but it isn't the aim. The writers of the Bible seem to want to go and be with Christ the way the most intimate and passionate lovers, when separated, desire their reunion.

In this way, Christ is our Juliet. What we feel for Him now is but a shadow of what we will feel for Him in His glory. If you can imagine the greatest love of your life, multiplied by millions, speaking affirmation into your soul, you will have in your mind the awareness of Christ and the community of the Trinity. All the self-awareness that occurred to us in God's absence will dissolve as Christ's love tells us who we are. In His presence we will not hate ourselves, second-guess ourselves, or compare ourselves to others; but rather, our lives will be filled with the gratitude of His presence, and we will know for the first time the glory of being human. Just as each member of the Trinity is thankful for the others, just as it was in the Garden between man and his Maker, it will be between you and me, and between us and the Godhead.

As such, there is still great trouble between Romeo and Juliet. While their love has been expressed, a certain poetic agreement has been made: The two cannot be unified because of the enduring strife between their families. They are still, for allegorical purposes, sludging their way through a fallen system. In this way, you and I must be unified with Christ in His death, and only in our actual deaths will we go and be with Him.

Our spirituality would indicate that when man sinned against God, the wages of sin was death because, as has been said, no life can exist outside God, as He is the author and giver of life. Scripture indicates Christ took the sin of the world upon Himself and was crucified on a cross to satisfy God's necessary wrath toward that which is evil. He did this, Scripture says, because He loves us. As we die to ourselves, doff our names, we find He gives Himself to us just as Juliet to Romeo and we become one with Him, so that, like a couple newly married, God looks at us and sees one Being, His Son, united, as it were, with His bride, alive in His purity, just as Romeo was made new by Juliet. Christ's death, again, was not a technicality by which we are covered with grace, but rather a passionate and inconceivable act of kindness and altruism and love stemming from God's desire to be reunited with His creation.

In keeping with the biblical narrative, Shakespeare painfully demands the couple's ultimate unity take place in their deaths. The two have tried at length to be together, but the rage between the families only intensifies as the play carries on toward its tragic end. A trick is planned: Juliet will fake her death, and the two will run off together. But Romeo is fooled by the seemingly dead body of his love, drinks from a poison himself, asking death to be the guide that leads him to his love. Slang during the Elizabethan period refers to sex as "one dying in the other," and Shakespeare has Romeo drink from a round cup, the symbol of a woman, and Juliet thrusting a dagger, a phallic symbol, into her chest. Two distinct sets of imagery are employed, the first being that of sex, or union, and the second being the Christian imagery of the church being united with Christ in His death.

In Baz Luhrmann's 1996 film *Romeo and Juliet*, starring Leonardo DiCaprio as Romeo and Claire Danes as Juliet, the director pays reverence to Shakespeare's use of Christian imagery and so sets crosses and icons in nearly every frame. And in this final and most meaningful scene of the play, Luhrmann sets the characters in a cathedral complete with neon crosses posted at each pew. Romeo walks the aisle as though he were the bride in a wedding, an aisle lit with candles that lead to Juliet's body, which is set on the altar like a sacrifice. It is here that Romeo takes his life to be with his love, and once awakened from her sleep, Juliet does the same. Their painful struggle is at an end as the two are thought to be united in heaven, where there is a wedding in waiting. The camera then lifts upward from the bodies to reveal Romeo and Juliet's tender limbs gently folded in an embrace, their forms laid amid a thousand burning candles that, as the camera lifts farther, reveal the image of a cross, the two lovers, finally together in peace, one purifying the other, now enjoying the beauty of their companionship uninterrupted by the enmity that once ripped them apart.

The last time I watched this dramatic scene unfold I was preparing a series of lectures on the theological implications of the play, considering all of this in academic terms. And yet as I did this, late in the evening and alone in my room, I was suddenly struck with the power of Paul's words in his letter to the Romans. I confess I was moved to tears at the implications of his statements, set in the context of a love story to explain all love stories. Paul would passionately present to the Romans these beautiful ideas:

> Since we have now been justified by his blood, how much more shall we be saved from God's wrath through him! (5:9 NIV)

> For if, when we were God's enemies, we were reconciled to him through the death of his Son, how much more, having been reconciled, shall we be saved through his life! (5:10 NIV)

> If we have been united with him like this in his death, we will certainly also be united with him in his resurrection. (6:5 NIV)

> If we died with Christ, we believe that we will also live with him. (6:8 NIV)

I had known in my head that these principles we understand, these beautiful theological ideas, were plot twists in a story of love, a story of God reaching out to mankind, but I don't think it was until I watched that final scene of *Romeo and Juliet*, with Paul's letter to the Romans open on my desk, that our spirituality was in fact a love story for me. This letter was God whispering in my ear that I no longer had to perform in a circus, I no longer had to defend myself in the sinking lifeboat, that God had come to earth, made Himself human, taken the world's sin upon Himself, and was crucified for me, so that His glory could shine through me, and I could be made whole.

And I go back to Eden, in my mind, to imagine what it is going to be like for you and me in heaven. I suppose it will be a new and marvelous paradise, where love will exist in its purest form, where the beauty of diversity will be understood for the first time, where self-hatred will fade into an agreement with God about the splendor of His creation, where physical beauty will no longer be used as a commodity, where you and I will feel free in our sincere love for others, ourselves, and God. And I suppose it will be in heaven that you and I actually understand each other, all the drama of the lifeboat a distant memory, all the arguments we had seeming so inconsequential, and the glory of God before us in all His majesty, shining like sunlight through our souls. This will be a good thing, my friend.

The lifeboat system of redemption seems so ugly in comparison to the love of God. We can trust our fate to a jury of peers in the lifeboat, we can work to accumulate wealth, buy beauty under a surgeon's knife, panic for our identities under the fickle friendship of culture, and still die in separation from the one voice we really needed to hear.

To me, it is more beautiful to trust Christ, deny our fathers and refuse our names, die to ourselves and live again in Him, raised up in the wave of His resurrection, baptized and made new in the purity of His righteousness. I hope you will join me in clinging to Him.

Time, which was God's friend, is now His enemy, and you and I are going to end with it soon. If you will lift a glass of wine with me, I would like to remember Him: Here is to Christ for making us, to Christ for rescuing us, and to Christ, who gives hope for tomorrow.

O true apothecary! Thy drugs are quick.

AFTERWORD

Concern may be felt by the reader for my lack of explaining the holiness of Christ and the degree to which His necessary death served as a propitiation for God's wrath on humanity. While I certainly agree these ideas are critical, true, and quite beautiful, my aim was to present an explanation of the gospel in relational language, dealing primarily with the story from which our theology has been deduced. In this way, this effort might be read as an apologetic, leaning on personality and culture more than math and logic, though I don't feel any of these ideas are less than logical.

I did wish, however, to pull our understanding of the gospel of Jesus out of the formulaic, propositional framework from which it has been sunk and return it, at least to some degree, into the world our broken biochemistry has created. That said, some thinkers may contend I believe systematic theology is the enemy, but this is not true. I find it a helpful guide and certainly recommend the study of systematic theology to enhance and explain, but not to replace, the human story. I appreciate your patience and kindness with any resistance I may have expressed in delineating one from the other.

THE GENESIS THEORY

WHY PEOPLE DO WHAT THEY DO

The early chapters of Genesis have interested me for a long time. They are rich from many perspectives: as literature, poetry, history, and truth. And the more I've thought about those passages, the more I'm convinced they offer something of a "personality theory," a way for each of us to understand ourselves in light of theology and the events of human history. What the world offers is an explanation of *what* we do. Genesis provides an understanding of *why* we do.

What follows is a summary of precepts I'm calling "The Genesis Theory" to explain the distinction between the *what* and the *why*. The theory, as I present it here, is going to be woefully incomplete, which is kind of on purpose. I'm hoping greater minds will expand upon it, criticize it, and refine the ideas. Biblical scholars have yet to present a comprehensive personality theory, and I think we've left a gap in the world of ideas by never producing one. I'm hoping this will get us going in the right direction.

In the account of the fall of man, the author of Genesis presents life before the fall and life after, and the difference is simply that before the fall, Adam and Eve walked around naked and felt no shame. After the fall they felt shame when naked. This, it seems, is the primary point of the passage, if for no other reason than the author repeats the fact several times.

Since the original publication of *Searching for God Knows What,* I've continued to think of Genesis 1 and 2 as the foundation for a personality theory. I don't believe this was the author's intent, but I do believe there is an answer to *why* we do what we do, something as meaningful as Freud or Maslow.

Certainly there are biological drives in play, the need for food and shelter and the innate desire to procreate, and so Genesis 1 and 2 do not explain everything, which, again, is not the intent of the text. However, seen through a certain lens, this brief bit of writing can offer a decently comprehensive explanation of our personalities.

This text is important because it provides the Christian answer to the most often asked question in our society, and that is, *what is wrong?* Every news channel, government, and country ballad is exploring this question.

The Christian answer, then, is simple. What is wrong with the world is that something happened that made human beings relationally incomplete and desperate to regain that relational completion, something so safe they felt no shame when naked.

While it may seem absurd or reductive that God only wants to show us the before-and-after of the fall as an explanation for millennia of searching and strife, when we break it down, it's quite a revealing explanation of human nature.

If you take out nude beaches and the few cultures where nudity is the norm, the idea that we feel shame when we are naked is pretty much universal. It is important to note that we are the *only* species to experience this phenomenon. To say this is true because it is inherent in our nature is too circular. I believe there must be a sociological or psychological reason that humans feel ashamed when naked, and these reasons serve as the starting point for the personality theory I think Genesis offers.

The Five Principles of The Genesis Theory

1. Humans look to something outside themselves to define and affirm their identity.
2. God gave humans the freedom to walk away.
3. There is a consequence to being outside of relationship with God.
4. In the absence of God, humans look to other relationships to define and affirm their intrinsic value.
5. Nobody but God has the agency to affirm the identity of humankind.

These five truths define why we do what we do, why we want what we want, speak the way we speak, daydream about what we daydream about, and fight over what we fight over. In other words, these five ideas, which I argue must be true in order for humans to feel shame when naked, give us a bedrock or an origin of who we are, a personality theory as comprehensive as any given by the founding fathers of psychology.

Here is how I see these five principles in a little more detail.

One: Humans look outside themselves to define and affirm their identity.

In the presence of God, man and woman could walk around naked and feel no shame. What this required was familiarity with the person looking on. Familiarity and trust. They believed this person was good, loving, kind, and accepting. God embodied and showed these traits so completely for the first humans that they were not self-aware in the way we are self-aware. This is God's original design. Humans, we can deduce then, were created to be in a relationship with God in which love and affirmation (strictly through God's presence) were given in a divine abundance and gave the ultimate sense of security. They did not feel shame. They did not have self-doubt. They felt their own completeness in the presence of God.

Two: God gave humans the freedom to turn away.

Forcing someone to love is not pure love. God had to give humankind the opportunity to turn away from Him in order to have an authentic love relationship. We chose to walk away from God.

Three: There is a consequence to being outside of relationship with God

Now, because humans were created to be in relationship with God, and they chose to break that relationship, what happened was death (or, eventual death). We might understand it better this way: As a flower is designed to be in relationship with the sun, humans were designed to be in relationship with God. What happens when a flower doesn't receive sunlight is the same thing that happens to humans—we do not have the most basic requirement for emotional well-being and life. This is the core of The Genesis Theory.

When we walked out of that safe relationship, we began to doubt we were loveable, safe, and secure. This happened because we all—that is, every human being on the planet—understand intuitively we are going to die unless something outside ourselves affirms us and tells us we are okay. We are designed to receive that only from God.

Four: In the Absence of God, Humans Looks to Other Relationships to Affirm Their Intrinsic Value.

As soon as God left, Adam and Eve immediately covered themselves. They felt shame for the first time. Most would argue that the reason they felt shame was because they had sinned against God. But that is only partly true. They felt shame because God was no longer there to affirm them. Adam and Eve wondered if they were good and secure because they knew they were outside a relational context with God.

Humans are designed to receive affirmation in relationship with God. Without that relationship, we look to other relationships to affirm our value. And to achieve that affirmation from our friends, neighbors, coworkers, family, and on and on . . . that need God originally fulfilled explains nearly everything about our personalities.

Five: Nobody but God Has the Agency to Affirm the Identity of Humankind.

Humans' use of others to affirm their intrinsic value does not work, except as a pacifier. By design, humans are to live in relationship with God, who, as the creator, has the agency to affirm their value with authority. Affirmation from other humans, then, while pacifying, has no real ability to complete our sense of wholeness and identity. "Lateral" affirmation from one another is insufficient, and it keeps us always longing for more.

The Genesis Theory and Human Personality

Apart from the biological functioning of humanity—that is, the desire to eat and procreate and protect ourselves—I believe these five points can explain our personalities quite comprehensively. The driving force is survival, for sure, but it's a different kind of survival than Darwinian survival. In Darwin's theories, enough should be enough. Once a person has food and can procreate, he should be satisfied. However, if what's at stake is the perceived value of a person's soul or our social standing we will continue to manipulate, impress, and embellish until we receive the amount of affirmation that brings a fleeting sense of completion. We do all this even after our basic needs are fulfilled. In the absence of God, we get people other than Him to say that we are okay. And this will, we think, free us from the consequences of our condition of separation from God.

The idea that we were designed for something outside ourselves to affirm our identity, and that there are consequences if we don't receive that affirmation, I'm convinced, helps explain disorders like separation anxiety, social phobia, narcissism, anxiety, dependent personalities, and anti-social personalities.

How The Genesis Theory Plays Out Practically

Over-obsession with romantic, intimate love. A person can believe that once they find a mate who loves and accepts them, they will be okay. This is irrational, of course. They will live for a span of years and die just like everybody else. Emotionally, this person's desire for love is actually a desire for the relationship that has the authority to define and affirm their identity and thus pacify them from the consequence of the fall.

Comparing and competition. In the absence of affirmation, we construct a perceived hierarchy amongst one another. Our survival mechanisms kick in, and we begin to compete with each other for the affirmation of the world. This is why people want to be famous, perhaps, and why those of us who are not famous want to associate with those who are. This also explains competitive sports and all forms of envy. (I expand on this in the lifeboat theory section of the book.)

Childhood security. Children who grow up in homes where they are affirmed and loved have a much greater chance at emotional health than those who don't. While human love is a pacifier against the inevitable consequence of God's absence, human love does have limited agency. Therefore, those who are consistently affirmed as children are less likely to desperately seek pacifying affirmations as adults. However, when the subconscious voice of the parent is misunderstood as the missing God-voice, the personality is corrupted.

The deceptive, image-making personality. If a person believes that other people's affirmations have the power to absolve the consequences of his or her nature, they will try to impress people by creating a false image (the equivalent of Adam and Eve covering with leaves) working endlessly on image, presenting a false self to the world.

Jealousy. Jealousy happens when we see somebody else getting the affirmation that we know we need to survive. If we did not need affirmation in order to survive, we would not get jealous.

Association/Dissociation. We associate ourselves with perceived winners and dissociate from perceived losers as a survival mechanism, aligning ourselves with those who are being affirmed from external sources.

Expanding upon the Theory in the Christian Classroom

The list of human emotions that can be explained through this theory is endless. I only offer this list as a beginning. Further expansion can be done by exploring the relationship between human emotions and the five principles involved in this theory.

Psychology classes can expand on this theory by asking the following questions:

1. Clarify and define the ideas involved in this theory. Should there be five? Should there be more or fewer? Is there language that could better define the ideas?
2. Define human dynamics using the five points. How exactly are some human emotions explained using the theory?

Clarification About the Gospel of Jesus and The Genesis Theory

Some will think the gospel of Jesus is the solution to the human personality, and to that I answer *sort of.*

By *sort of,* I really mean that a relationship with Jesus will ultimately reunite us with God, returning us to the One we were designed to be in relationship with, the missing piece in completing the human personality. But in Christian theology, so long as we are in the world, we will still live in a tension with our fallen nature (see Romans 7). In other words, Christ completes us sufficiently but our full restoration has not happened yet. The living Christian, in this regard, is in the same predicament as the non-Christian, still looking for affirmation from the world to pacify the soul. The Christian should, however, recognize three things:

1. They should understand that the pacifying affirmation of the world is without agency and has no real power to keep them alive.

2. They should practice patience through life, knowing that through Christ they will someday be reconciled to God.
3. They should understand why it is that people do what they do, understanding these things through the personality theory derived from Genesis 1 and 2.

Why Any of This Matters

The practical application for The Genesis Theory matters because it provides a framework to counsel people toward health, negotiate peace between warring nations, create economic equality, provide a system to understand our own emotional tension, and offer a hope that serves as a true and healthy pacifier until we are reunited with God.

If Christians can comprehensively understand the workings of the human personality, we can offer the world a degree of hope not available to the founding fathers of psychology. It is my hope that together we can build such a theory based on God's truth and His Word as a viable and life-giving alternative that our world so desperately needs. Again, I invite you to criticize and expand upon this theory to make it exactly that.

ABOUT THE AUTHOR

Donald Miller is the author of *Blue Like Jazz, Searching for God Knows What, Through Painted Deserts,* and *To Own a Dragon.* He is the founder of The Mentoring Project and serves on President Barack Obama's task force on Fatherlessness and Healthy Families. He lives and works in Portland, Oregon.

If you want to stay connected with Don, you can visit the following:

Blog
www.donmilleris.com

Twitter
@donmilleris

ACKNOWLEDGMENTS

This book is dedicated to my friend John MacMurray, who, for many years, led a college Bible study at Good Shepherd Community Church outside Portland. John is a terrific Bible teacher, and much of the thinking in this book was stimulated during the four years I lived with him and his family. I am certain there are hundreds more former students of John's who also wish to express their appreciation to him for his commitment to truth and meaning and especially to the endearing nature of Jesus. John, I can't thank you and Terri enough for your kindness and willingness to share your love for God's Word and His people. You deserve a better book than this.

I would once again like to thank Kathy Helmers for her faith in this project and her encouragement. I owe a great deal of thanks to Lee Hough for his kindness and diligence in making sure I completed the manuscript. Brian Hampton and Kyle Olund were incredibly patient, and their encouragement and advice shaped and reshaped the book into something readable. The people at Thomas Nelson Publishers are of the greatest quality people I know, to a person, and I am thankful for their friendship. These kind people are: publisher Jonathan Merkh, as well as Kathleen Crow, Carol Martin, Jerry Park, Pamela Clements, Belinda Bass, Paula Major, Ashley Aiken, Danielle Douglas (with the help of Deonne and Rachel), Blythe McIntosh, Brandi Lewis, Gary Davidson, Scott Harvey, Ron Land, Dave Shepherd, Carolyn Beckham, college intern David Lavender, and veteran acquisitions editor Victor Oliver, who, although I've never met him, has sold copies of *Blue Like Jazz* by the carton out of his trunk.

I am grateful to my friend Tony Kriz, who, during dozens of long conversations, listened carefully, adding, clarifying and criticizing thoughts, helping to mold the ideas into communicable forms.

John Sailhamer's thoughts and teaching were remarkable and stimulated many of these ideas (specifically on truth and meaning and the writings of Moses), and his book *The Pentateuch as Narrative* is a terrific place to start learning about finding meaning in the Bible. Thanks to Daniel Goleman and Richard Dawkins, who got me thinking about personality, community, trends, and *The Selfish Gene.* I also found Portland writer Katherine Dunn's treatment of circus life in *Geek Love* moving, beautiful, dark, and profound; I enjoyed the writings of Martin Luther and John Calvin as well. There are a great many books about *Romeo and Juliet,* but there aren't many critics who are willing to say Shakespeare intended the balcony scene as a metaphor for conversion. I cannot see the text any other way, and I trust that even a casual reader will find more theology than romance in the ideas spoken in the Capulet courtyard. Forgive me, however, if I have failed objectivity. If these ideas are true, however, Shakespeare was a kind of prophet in whose chest beat, perhaps, the poet heart of Luther himself. And if I am wrong, then I still find it beautiful he borrowed from Christ's wanting of His bride to explain Juliet's wanting of Romeo.

I neglected friendships to write this book, and I am thankful for the patient love of the people I consider close: Much love and appreciation to Tony, Penny, Tuck, Laura Long, Leslie Mckellar, and Rick McKinley. And I would like to thank the guys at Testosterhome, who make coming home like finding peace. Those guys are Stacy, Wes, Grant, and Blake. And special thanks to the folks at Imago Dei, whom I love with all my heart. (Rick McKinley's book *Jesus in the Margins* (published in 2005 is a good read. Check out Rick's thoughts about Jesus.) I want to thank Robin Jones Gunn, Brian McLaren, and Chris Seay for their encouragement and advice about writing and for being such good people.

And a giant, loving, special thank you to Kurt and Donna Nelson, who, together, are the Mark Moskowitz in my life. (See the documentary *Stone Reader* for an explanation.)

This book was written under mood music provided by Patty Griffin, Lou Reed, The Shins, The Smiths, Derek Webb, Robert Keen, Steve Earle, Andrew Peterson, The Indigo Girls, Beck, Sinead O'Connor, David Wilcox, Joseph Arthur, Bebo Norman, Pedro the Lion, Soundgarden, The Trash Can Sinatras, Pat Green, The Rolling "you can't always get what you want" Stones, Nickel Creek, Climber, Damien Rice, The Frames, and The Be Good Tanya's. Thanks for taking us to places words don't know how to go.

Much thanks to Palio coffee, the shops in the Pearl, and Powell's Books for warm, dry spaces and coffee. And as always, the city of Portland for having the best bus system in the States, and for going its own direction to become one of the greatest places in the world in which to live. And a special thank you to all the Imago Starbucks bums, ever blowing air into coffee, ever making community a reality and caffeine jitters a wiring through which we interpret life. *Am I talking too fast?*

I also want to thank you for reading this book. It means a great deal that you would sit and listen, and I am grateful for the e-mails and stories. I do hope you find all the beauty of life wrapped up in the person and message of Christ. God be with you on this journey. We will see you on the other side.

An excerpt from Donald Miller's

A Million Miles in a Thousand Years

one

Random Scenes

THE SADDEST THING about life is you don't remember half of it. You don't even remember half of half of it. Not even a tiny percentage, if you want to know the truth. I have this friend Bob who writes down everything he remembers. If he remembers dropping an ice cream cone on his lap when he was seven, he'll write it down. The last time I talked to Bob, he had written more than five hundred pages of memories. He's the only guy I know who remembers his life. He said he captures memories, because if he forgets them, it's as though they didn't happen; it's as though he hadn't lived the parts he doesn't remember.

I thought about that when he said it, and I tried to remember something. I remembered getting a merit badge in Cub Scouts when I was seven, but that's all I could remember. I got it for helping a neighbor cut down a tree. I'll tell that to God when he asks what I did with my life. I'll tell him I cut down a tree and got a badge for it. He'll most likely want to see the merit badge, but I lost it years ago, so when I'm done with my story, God will probably sit there looking at me, wondering what to talk about next. God and Bob will probably talk for days.

I know I've had more experiences than this, but there's no way I can remember everything. Life isn't memorable enough to remember everything. It's not like there are explosions happening all the time or dogs smoking cigarettes. Life is slower. It's like we're all watching a movie, waiting for something to happen, and every couple months the audience points at the screen and says, "Look, that guy's getting a parking ticket." It's strange the things we remember.

I tried to remember more and made a list, and it pretty much amounted to the times I won at something, the times I lost at something, childhood dental appointments, the first time I saw a girl with her shirt off, and large storms.

• • •

After trying to make a list of the things I remembered, I realized my life, for the most part, had been a series of random experiences. When I was in high school, for example, the homecoming queen asked me for a kiss. And that year I scored the winning touchdown in a game of flag football; the guys in the tuba section beat the girls in the clarinet section twenty-one to fourteen. A year or so later I beat my friend Jason in tennis, and he was on the tennis team. I bought a new truck after that. And once at a concert, my date and I snuck back-stage to get Harry Connick Jr.'s autograph. He'd just married a Victoria's Secret model, and I swear she looked at my hair for an inappropriate amount of time.

The thing about trying to remember your life is it makes you wonder what any of it means. You get the feeling life means something, but you're not sure what. Life has a peculiar feel when you look back on it that it doesn't have when you're actually living it.

Sometimes I'm tempted to believe life doesn't mean anything at all. I've read philosophers who say meaningful experiences are purely subjective, and I understand why they believe that, because you can't prove life and love and death are anything more than random happenings. But then you start thinking about some of the scenes you've lived, and if you've had a couple of drinks, they have a sentimental quality that gets you believing we are all poems coming out of the mud.

The truth is, life could be about any number of things. Several years ago, my friends Kyle and Fred were visiting Oregon, for instance, and we drove into the desert and climbed Smith Rock. There were forest fires in the Cascade Range that summer, so a haze had settled in the Columbia River Gorge. The smoke came down the river and bulged a deeper gray between the mountains. When the sun went down, the sky lit up like Jesus was coming back. And when the color started happening, my friends and I stopped talking. We sat and watched for the better part of an hour and later said we'd not seen anything better. I wondered then if life weren't about nature, if we were supposed to live in the woods and grow into the forest like tree moss.

But that same year I met a girl named Kim who didn't wear any shoes. She was delightful and pretty, and even during the Oregon winter she walked from her car to the store in bare feet, and through the aisles of the store and in the coffee shops and across the cold, dirty floor at the post office. I liked her very much. One night while looking at her, I wondered if life was about romantic affection, about the thing that gets exchanged between a man and a woman. Whatever I felt for Kim, I noted, I didn't feel for tree moss.

And when my friends Paul and Danielle had their second daughter, I went to the hospital and held her in my arms. She was tiny and warm like a hairless cat, and she was dependent. When I looked over at her mother, Danielle's eyes told me life was about more than sunsets and romance. It was as though having a baby made all the fairy tales come true for her, as though she were a painter who discovered a color all new to the world.

I can imagine what kind of conversation God and Danielle will have, how she'll sit and tell God the favorite parts of the story he gave her. You get a feeling when you look back on life that

that's all God really wants from us, to live inside a body he made and enjoy the story and bond with us through the experience.

Not all the scenes in my life have been pleasant, though, and I'm not sure what God means with the hard things. I haven't had a lot of hard things happen, not like you see on the news; and the hard memories I've had seem like random experiences. When I was nine, for instance, I ran away from home. I ran as far as the field across the street where I hid in the tall grass. My mother turned on the porch light and got in the car and drove to McDonald's and brought back a Happy Meal. When she got home, she held the McDonald's bag high enough I could see it over the weeds. I followed the bag down the walkway to the door, and it shone under the porch light before it went into the house. I lasted another ten minutes. I sat quietly at the table and ate the hamburger while my mother sat on the couch and watched television. Neither of us said anything. I don't know why I remember that scene, but I do. And I remember going to bed feeling like a failure, like a kid who wasn't able to run away from home.

Most of the painful scenes in my life involve being fat. I got fat as a kid and got fatter as an adult. I had a girlfriend out of high school who wanted to see me with my shirt off, but I couldn't do it. I knew if she saw me she would leave. She wouldn't leave right then, but she would leave when she found a nobler reason. She never did, but I never took my shirt off either. I'd kiss down her neck, and she'd reach into my shirt, and I'd pull her hand down, then lose concentration. I suppose a therapist would say this memory points to something, but I don't know what it points to. I don't have a therapist.

When I was in high school, we had to read *The Catcher in the Rye* by J. D. Salinger. I liked the book, but I don't know why. I go back to read it sometimes, but now it annoys me. But I still remember scenes. I remember Holden Caulfield in the back of a taxi, asking the driver where the ducks in Central Park go in the winter. And I remember the nuns asking for donations. I remember the last scene in the book, too, when you realize he'd been telling the story to a counselor in a nuthouse. I wonder if that's what we'll do with God when we are through with all this, if he'll show us around heaven, all the light coming in through windows a thousand miles away, all the fields sweeping down to a couple of chairs under a tree, in a field outside the city. And we'll sit and tell him our stories, and he'll smile and tell us what they mean.

I just hope I have something interesting to say.